WITH HOPE IN THEIR EYES

VIVIENNE FRANCIS

Published by Nia, an imprint of The X Press
6 Hoxton Square, London N1 6NU
Tel: 0171 729 1199
Fax: 0171 729 1771

Printed by Caledonian International Book Manufacturing Ltd, Glasgow, UK.

Distributed in US by INBOOK, 1436 West Randolph Street, Chicago, Illinois 60607,
USA Orders 1-800 626 4330 Fax orders 1-800 334 3892

Distributed in UK by Turnaround Distribution, Unit 3, Olympia Trading Estate,
Coburg Road, London N22 6TZ
Tel: 0181 829 3000
Fax: 0181 881 5088

ISBN 1-874509-65-4

ABOUT THE AUTHOR

Twenty-five year old Vivienne Francis was born in London of Caribbean parents. She has worked as a newspaper reporter, and is currently a radio broadcaster with the BBC. *With Hope In Their Eyes* is her first book.

INTRODUCTION

When the Empire Windrush anchored at Tilbury Docks in Kent, June 22 1948, few on board could have imagined their arrival was to shape the course of British history. Although there was already a small black presence in Britain, the ship's arrival heralded an unprecedented wave of post-war immigration from the Caribbean. Four hundred and ninety two West Indians disembarked from the Empire Windrush. A decade later, nearly 125,000 had made a similar journey across the Atlantic to the "motherland".

This informative and compelling fly-on-the-wall tribute is a compilation of the true life stories of those early black settlers who made the voyage and paved the way for future generations.

Even now, as the Empire Windrush generation celebrates its golden anniversary, many of those early settlers are only just coming to terms with the last fifty years of life in Britain. Once they stepped on that ship to England, the lives of these ordinary black men and women became anything but ordinary. Time and time again during the course of my research, the pioneers included in this book described their fifty years in Britain as one long dream (sometimes sweet, but mostly a nightmare), as they considered whether it had all been worth it.

The Windrush generation left their homeland for a

multitude of reasons. Some sought fortune and truly believed the streets were paved with gold; others sought to take advantage of England's seemingly superior educational system; some travelled for the sheer adventure of it; and there were those guided by Cupid's dart, obediently following the dreams of their husbands or boyfriends. At a time when Britannia ruled the waves and the 'superiority' of all things white was drilled into the black Caribbean consciousness, who could blame them for crossing the ocean to England?

Those few who had already ventured to England, serving king and country during the Second World War, knew what to expect. However, most arrived in summer suits and flimsy clothing, ill-prepared for what was in store for them. But all of them — men, women and children — came with open hearts and hope in their wide eyes.

Fifty years on, hope remains in the eyes of these early settlers, despite the slings and arrows of outrageous prejudice they have had to endure in Britain. It is difficult for me, the second generation of Caribbean migrants, to imagine that the British Government, which had been only too happy for black men and women to bolster the armed forces during the war, would tolerate signs such as *No Blacks, No Irish, No Dogs* at home and in the workplace. The great irony, of course, is that the Commonwealth migrants were invited to Britain to help with the labour shortage after the war. The tide quickly turned and the invitation was revoked.

Faced with the hostile climate, it would have been easy for the Windrush generation to cut their losses, pack their bags and return home. Some did. But the majority stayed. For a people of strength and courage, adversity often sparks the greatest triumphs. The sons, daughters and grandchildren of the Windrush generation now reap the rewards of this resilience.

Fifty years after the arrival of the Empire Windrush, there is now a significant black influence on British culture, politics, sport and academia. Despite the tiring problems we face every day, we are barristers, accountants, head teachers, professors, surgeons, pilots, bankers — in fact, we can be found in all corners of British life. Thanks to the Windrush generation who laid the foundation, it is even possible to conceive of a black British prime minister in the near future.

Some of the early settlers whose true stories I have documented in *With Hope In Their Eyes*, are content to see their last days in England, while many of them are joyfully packing their bags to finally return home to their island in the sun. For others, hampered by age or financial instability, this prospect is destined to remain a dream to which they cling in vain. Yet, there is no sadness in their stories. *With Hope In Their Eyes* is nothing but uplifting throughout.

Told in their own words, some of the stories are so unbelievable that the powerful narrative of these early settlers reads like a bestselling novel. *With Hope In Their Eyes* is, however, too real to be fiction. *With Hope In Their Eyes* tells it like it REALLY was.

VIVIENNE FRANCIS, APRIL 1998, LONDON.

Acknowledgements:
ANDRE SHERVINGTON, BEN BOUSQUET, CONNIE MARKS, CECIL HOLNESS, NORMAN PHILLIPS, DORIS RANKIN, IO SMITH, CLARENCE THOMPSON, KELVIN COOK-MOHAMMED, WINSTON STAFFORD-HUSBAND, GLORIA BAILEY, ROBERT MURRAY, LEN GARRISON, GEORGE POWE, SMOKEY JOE, INTIUS MCPHERSON, CAPTAIN FISH, TIMOTHY COOPER, ASTON FERGUSON, MUM and DAD. FINALLY, BIG THANKS TO DOTUN.

PROLOGUE

492 MEN ON THE SHIP OF GOOD HOPE

What were they thinking these 492 Jamaicans, as the Empire Windrush slid upstream with the flood between the closing shores of Kent and Essex?

Standing by the rail this morning high above the landing-stage at Tilbury, one of them looked over the unlovely town to the grey-green fields beyond and said, 'If this is England I like it'. A good omen, perhaps. May he and his friends suffer no sharp disappointment.

MANCHESTER GUARDIAN, JUNE 23, 1948

"Land, land. Me see England." The words were so few, but they symbolised so much.

It was dark and misty, on the brink of daybreak, as the mighty Empire Windrush majestically cut through the grey murky river towards Tilbury, its final destination. Twenty three year old Timothy Cooper, a young Jamaican, had finally arrived in Great Britain, the Motherland.

He was just one of the hundreds of West Indians jostling for position on board, hoping to steal a glimpse of land over the heads and shoulders of those few who had clinched the prime positions. Some of the more eager perched precariously on fragile suitcases, others carefully hoisted their bodies up ropes and poles dotted around the upper deck.

Peering between the swarm of passengers, Timothy, or T as he preferred to be called, could just make out the outline of the coast. He was weary from the long journey, but the sight of land lifted his spirit. This was England, the land where he would be judged on his merits. The land where, if he worked hard, he would achieve. The land that had so much to offer. The promised land.

Far into the barren green landscape, endless mounds of hills dotted with small buildings puffed out clouds of smoke.

"What a load of factories. Surely we must get a job at one of them," T assured himself as he turned the collar of his coat up, trying to get a little protection from the biting chill. Cold though it was, his freezing body was thawed by the inner glow that he felt inside.

It had been a slow, painstaking voyage. The old British freighter had never really picked up much pace. Four weeks was a long time to stay on a boat, especially on a voyage of this magnitude. Fortunately the journey had not been without excitement.

T cast his mind back to his home, the rich, sunny isle of Jamaica, where it had all began.

T's Story

One of the largest batches of passengers to leave Jamaica in peace time will sail this morning when the troop ship Empire Windrush leaves port on a long voyage to England, taking a total of 900 passengers from Kingston.

During its three days at port, the Windrush became easily the most popular ship that has docked in Kingston harbour for a long time. The Royal Mail Wharf was a scene of activity and animation as sailing preparations proceeded.
DAILY GLEANER **27 MAY 1948**

It had all started as a rumour, the type that was enticing to hear, but no-one really paid any mind to. It was only when T Cooper saw the advertisements in the Daily Gleaner newspaper that he believed what the gossips were saying.

A boat was going to England and Jamaicans, as long as they had a valid passport, a signature from a

Justice of the Peace saying they were a responsible citizen and a signature from the police stating that they were not a criminal, could get a passage for 28 pounds 10 shillings. It was a lot of money for an average Jamaican, but a fraction of the cost of the usual fare to England.

T did not care much for going so far away from his family, but there was the promise of work in England. "Six jobs for one man," a friend had told him. With that T made up his mind. He would go, stay a few years, earn some money then come back home a rich man.

T was twenty three. He was from the country — St Catherine's. He lived in a small two-roomed wooden house with a red galvanised roof, outside toilet and tin bath. They relied on the drain in the roof to collect the water. He shared the house with his mother and eight brothers. His father had died some years earlier.

T was a cultivator by trade, earning most of his living from the giant rows of bamboo-like sugar cane that surrounded his dwelling. Each year when the cane had matured, T would go through the same ritual: At dawn he would ignite the undergrowth to scare away snakes and rodents that might be lurking. Then, with a freshly sharpened cutlass, hastily hack away at the crop while his brothers stacked the cut cane into tidy bundles on a cart.

When the heat from the sun became too intense, T sat under a coconut tree sipping lime juice and handing out fat strips of the pale sugar cane nectar to the local children who conveniently wandered by to satisfy their palates. T would also put some of the sugar cane aside for his mother to make cane juice.

As well as cutting sugar cane, T could also earn a decent living from selling oranges and bananas that he picked from the fertile neighbouring land. Like other farmers in the village, he would lay his goods out on the dusty ground in front of his home. The checker would come from Kingston periodically and pick out what he wanted to buy. Once his mule was loaded with produce, the checker would make his way back along the cobbled track to the centre of the village.

But in 1948, business was not going so well for Jamaica's farmers. The great hurricane of 1944 had already dealt them a cruel hand and, now, the post-war world economies had no need or money to buy what they had to sell. Britain, the motherland, was concerned with rebuilding its infrastructure and exports, not in supporting Jamaican farmers.

The 1944 hurricane. Days before the winds came, the chickens wandered around the yard, scratching the dry earth, with an uneasy nervousness.

Then came the forecasters predictions in news flashes on the wireless. For those without such luxuries, local police personally delivered the message. Houses were boarded up and those who could, went to stay with friends and relatives in stronger dwellings in the town. Then it came.

At first it was barely a trickle of water and a gentle rustle of wind. But these were merely the foot soldiers who eventually made way for the entire regiment of wind and rain. A gradual darkness consumed the light of day. The hiss of the wind ripened into a chorus of howls. Heavy rain fell from the sky and gigantic waves lashed the coastline into submission.

Anything that stood in the hurricane's path was furiously uprooted and cast aside. Centuries old trees, family homes that had housed four generations, prized motor vehicles — everything was destroyed.

It was one of the worst storms Jamaica had seen. On T's own land, so much of the crop had been wiped out by the torrential rains and winds that there was little to salvage. The bananas were tiny, stunted in their growth, and their sharp green hue had been replaced by battered black speckles. Only one of the orange trees was left standing. It would take years to replace them.

The price of everything had plummeted. Now when the checker came, he would look on the humble offerings and frown. T needed to sell stacks of boxes of bananas and oranges just to earn a few cents. The fall in demand meant that so much went to waste: T was left with mounds and mounds of produce that eventually wilted away. Coffee and chocolate sold a little better, as they could be kept in storage in Kingston until the market picked up and a boat eventually came from overseas to collect the produce.

Yes, England would be different. T had heard that the war had killed off a lot of the working population, and industry was crying out for good men.

T was no stranger to working overseas. When he was nineteen, he had gone to the United States to try his luck there. He had ended up in Wisconsin with twenty other Jamaicans, where they cultivated corn, peas and carrots for a rich land owner.

After the season finished the foreman said they would keep ten of the workers, but the men had to sort it out amongst themselves which of them would stay and which would go.

T had worked hard and kept out of trouble. His good track record compelled the foreman to try and persuade him to stay.

But T chose to leave. Five of the men he knew from his district were moving on, and for a Jamaican far away from home in a white man's land, it did not make sense him staying on his own.

After a long train journey, they ended up in Arizona, cotton picking. But there was not much money or work, so they ended up back in Virginia then cut their losses and returned home. T later found out that those who had stayed in Wisconsin had remained there for three years. He had made the wrong decision.

But other than America, T knew little about the outside world, except that the rest of the world was where "English man ruled". So he might as well go to the home of the ruler.

Dawn had just broke at the Royal Mail Wharf in Harbour Street. Kingston was a busy Caribbean port with all kinds of vessels coming in and out — from huge gleaming steam ships to dwarf-like handcrafted wooden boats and rafts that in comparison barely seemed seaworthy.

Some were piled high with sacks of coffee,
chocolate and barrels of fresh fruits being transported
to distant lands. Others carrying the humble wares of
local fishermen.

The crude stench of oil oozing from the vessels and
the potent odour of fish permeated the salty air. Birds
hovered trying to steal discarded scraps from the
fisherman returning from a long day's work.

At the end of the long pier, a grand old trooper ship
stood silently on the quay. It had arrived from the
Middle East. Like a gigantic white wedding cake, it
was made up of many layers. At its base, four rows of
port holes decorated its smooth off-white sides.
Symmetrically between the round holes, were the bold
letters 'Empire Windrush, London'. Further up, lines
of lifeboats swung gently in the breeze. Then the final
touches, two funnels positioned on top like candles.
This was the vessel that was going to change lives and
fortunes. Its importance was such that the military
and local police had been assigned to watch over the
ship.

It was early, yet a flock from all corners of the
island, dressed in Sunday best — trilbies, suits and
ties for the men, frilly starched dresses for the women
— had already begun to assemble. Some were saying
goodbye to loved ones who were leaving to make the
long voyage to England. Others were standing in line,
ready for a long wait, hoping for a place on the ship
that would take them there — the Empire Windrush.

A stout, ebony-coloured woman sat proudly on the
stone wall. As she tried desperately not to crumple her
crimson flared dress, the circles of perspiration that

had stained the arms of the frock multiplied.

Using her plump forearm to wipe trickles of sweat from her glistening forehead, she called out to a group of small children playing near one of the docked boats.

"Hattie. Charles. Stop it, you hear. Or me going lick yuh backside."

Just a few yards away, under a palm tree, a young man resting his head on a battered old tan suitcase with a string tied around it. His fawn-coloured trilby hat was perched over his face, blocking out the beam of the morning sun.

The pretty girl sitting next to him tried to get his attention, gently stroking his hand and whispering in his ear. But the man appeared to pay her no mind. He had happily succumbed to the call of sleep.

T Cooper had left home early to guarantee his place on the Windrush. The night before he had laid out his prized navy suit — the new style with slit pockets, peg-top trousers and a red and gold tie and trilby hat to finish the ensemble off nicely. He then counted out the money he had saved for the journey. It only amounted to a couple of pounds, but his mother had emptied her emergency box and given him the contents. T vowed to pay her back many times over once he started work in England.

Countless times during his long sleepless night, T had heard his mother get up to pack and re-pack his old brown suitcase just to make sure her son would arrive in England fully prepared.

Before sunrise, a neighbour gave T and his mother

a lift to town in his pick-up truck. Once at Harbour Street, T joined the line and settled, anticipating a long wait.

"Boy, T you going to England too?" It was James Baker. He lived in the same district, St Catherine's.

"Yeah man. Me going to try me luck, y'know. Me never know you were going, though."

"Well, life has been hard. Me nuh work fe nearly a year and Ella just have a child. Boy, me is going to miss her, you know."

"Yeah, man."

"Well we'll catch up on the boat, me hope so. The line is long. A lot of people turn up. Me hope me get on," sighed James.

"Man, it a big ship, we will get on," T reassured.

As the hours passed, the numbers at the harbour grew and grew. It became a sea of eager faces, littered with suitcases and sealed boxes. Policemen paced up and down, seeking out any potential troublemakers. Every once in a while there would be a loud shrill as someone spotted a familiar face. Conversation was all about England and the travellers' expectations.

"Me hear England cold, but we going earn so much money we'll keep warm," boasted the cheerful travellers.

Some ate to pass the time away, suckling on roasted corn or jerk pork bought from the roadside vendors who started to assemble as news travelled that good business was to be had at Harbour Street that day.

It was almost midday. The sun was nearing its highest point in the sky and radiated an intense heat. For T, it seemed like an eternity waiting for the call to start boarding the Windrush. But at last the hour was upon him.

As the line began to filter through the gate of the landing stage, T picked up his suitcase and turned towards his mother.

"Make sure you write as soon as you get there," she smiled as she thrust a string bag stuffed with "not yet ready" mangoes, lime juice with sugar, just the way T liked it, and fresh bread.

"Of course, the moment me get there."

It was difficult for T to leave her. She was such a good woman. Since his father died T had vowed to support her. He could not wait until he reached England and was able to send her some proper money.

"Wrap up, because me hear England so cold. And don't forget to write." She repeated almost fearing this would be the last time she set eyes on her son.

"Me see you soon, don't worry. Me nuh stay long," promised T, sensing the urgency in her voice.

"Me hope so." Tears trickled down her pale honey-coloured cheeks.

Armed with minimal luggage, the Windrushians

painstakingly climbed the gangway to take up their positions on the boat, moving with such ponderousness as if they longed to steal a few more moments on familiar soil. The earlier expressions of excitement changed to anxiety. Below, those left behind wore an unmistakable sadness.

Military men stood at the foot of the gangplank rigorously inspecting travel documents, others roamed around the ship itself randomly questioning passengers. One man argued that he had lost his passport, saying that he had given it to a relative to hold for fear of being pickpocketed. Another tried to board using a friend's ticket and passport. Both men were escorted off the vessel.

As the funnel let out a loud groan then choked thick black smoke, T looked down to see if he could spot his mother. He could not make her out amongst all the hundreds of other faces. But he knew she was down there somewhere amidst the shouting and waving loved ones.

"Don't forget to write. I love you... Just mind yourself. Goodbye. Goodbye..." The voices echoed around the harbour.

After the last lucky passengers scrambled on, the footbridge was hoisted on board and they were off.

As the Windrush edged out into the Caribbean sea, Jamaica grew smaller and smaller until it became just a dot on the horizon.

T was sad to leave his paradise island; the sun-drenched golden beaches, aqua waters, the corn roasting on a hot iron rack by the roadside. The island where he could scale a coconut tree and suck out the bittersweet nectar of its juice. From the few people he knew that had been to England already, it had none of those things.

He found it hard to fight back the tears in his eyes. But T was not alone. Hundreds were on the deck saying their last farewell to the place they knew as home. No-one knew quite what lay ahead, but there was a common belief that it would be a better life than the one they were leaving behind.

But amidst all the sentimentality, the Windrushians had to be practical. Within the complex web of narrow corridors and decks, each needed somewhere to sleep. The sparse cabins had rows of bunk beds, enough for ten men. But the crew had warned that they would probably have to make room for more, as so many had wanted to travel.

Some were forced to lay their heads wherever they could find space. Once he had found a place to sleep, T began to explore the creaking, old vessel that would be his home for the next twenty or so days.

A number of stowaways succeeded in getting on board and mingling with the men. Although no definite figures are available, it appears that they number in the region of 20. A few of them have already been prosecuted and fined and imprisoned at Gravesend.
COLONIAL OFFICE 30 JUNE 1948

STOWAWAY ON BOARD

Most of the married men had left their partners and children at home, and hoped to send for them later. Only five complete families sailed. Two of the wives are Englishwomen who followed their husbands to Jamaica and now return with them to England. One of them, Mrs Doreen Zayne, formerly, and soon to be once more, of Blackpool confessed that she did not care for Jamaica and was glad to be going home again. She has two children, a boy and girl. Her husband hopes to find work in Lancashire.
MANCHESTER GUARDIAN JUNE 23 1948

"Me is not a stowaway," a voice shrilled. "Me come on to do the laundry. Me's a washer woman. Me . . . "

"But how come you still here? What happen?" A man's voice quickly interjected.

About an hour into the journey, T noticed some commotion between five or six men. There was a black woman on the boat. She was young, dressed in crumpled, dirty clothes, and her hair was covered with a multicoloured head scarf. T had not seen any other women since he had boarded. Apart from a handful of white women who were accompanying their ex-service husbands back home.

A small crowd of passengers had now gathered in one of the passages of the lower deck to hear the woman's story.

"Me was late getting back and before me had a chance to get off, me hear the boat leaving. Me is not a stowaway. Please don't let the captain find me, they'll put me in jail. Me is an honest woman. Me never want go ah England."

"Well don't worry, we will help you," assured several of the men.

It was agreed that the woman would be hidden away.

The first stop was Tampico, Mexico. The Windrush stayed docked in the harbour for a night and a day and picked up some produce for the long Atlantic stretch of the journey. It then stopped in Bermuda for three days. It was a strange experience for many of the Windrushians who had never ventured outside Jamaica.

Bermuda was one of the few Caribbean islands to still have an active, legitimate colour bar. In the shops, the black Windrushians were not served, and in the picture house, they were made to sit at the back. A few of the men got into fights over this blatant discrimination.

T felt sympathy for the men he met in Bermuda

who wanted to stowaway on the Windrush and try
their luck in England.

"Come. If we go on the ship and collect some of the
passes, then bring them out to you, they'll let you on.
Nuh worry," he reassured.

Once on board, the stowaways mixed quite easily
with the other passengers, who felt that they had just
as much right to be there as everyone else, even
though they had not paid the fare.

"T, T, T, they find her . . . they find her," Frank burst
into the cabin.

"Who? What?" questioned T, stretching out of his
sleep and struggling to sit up in the narrow bunk bed.

"The Kingston washerwoman . . . the Captain find
her," shouted Frank. "Some of the lads are collecting
some money to pay her fare. We can't let these people
think she's a stowaway. T, where's your money?"

Quickly a hat was circulated and the woman's fare
was raised. Soon after the captain whisked her away
to another part of the ship. T did not hear of her again.

ROBERT'S STORY

I understand that your Department is already aware of the fact that a very large number of Jamaican workers are expected to arrive in this country on the Empire Windrush due at Tilbury.

We are very worried about their accommodation upon arrival. It is estimated that, although a small number of the men will have friends here and so might be accommodated, between 300/375 will have nowhere to go. Is it possible for your Department to help us through the medium of the National Hostels Corporation?

I am sure you will appreciate the political importance of seeing that everything possible is done to assist them. We must therefore see that the smoothest possible arrangements are made to minimise the risk of any undesirable incidents or complaints that the Mother Country does not look after coloured Colonial British subjects.

COLONIAL OFFICE **JUNE 1948**

Robert Murray had read in the paper about a boat called the Empire Windrush, coming from Jamaica carrying four hundred West Indians.

"These people are going to make life in England worse for us," thought Robert. He believed that the few black men and women who had been in the Royal Air force and fought for the British Empire were just beginning to get accepted. Although there were one or two who demanded to know when Robert was going back to where he came from, by and large, the English were grateful for their contribution to the war effort and went out of their way to make them feel welcome.

But more black people would "clutter up the place and it would work to our detriment," Robert warned his friends. He saw himself and other ex-Royal Air Force men as the elite and that these other Jamaicans coming would drag them down.

Robert was nineteen years old when he left British Guiana for England in 1943 with the Royal Air Force to fight in the war. His father had not liked the idea, but Robert had made his mind up. He wanted adventure and excitement. One or two of his friends were also going so that made it more the better.

When Robert had left school, his father had put him through various trades — tailoring, cabinet making, diamond cutting — things which he proved to have no aptitude for.

Then one sticky Sunday afternoon, Robert was sitting on his front door step of the old house in Bent Street listening to some music on the wireless. Suddenly the broadcast was interrupted by a news flash. Marshall music blasted through the tiny speaker signalling that something important was to follow.

"I'm speaking to you from the Cabinet room of number 10 Downing Street." It was Prime Minister Neville Chamberlain.

"This morning the British Ambassador in Germany handed the German government a note stating that unless they withdraw their troops from Poland by 11 o'clock, a state of war will commence between us. I have to tell you now that no such undertaking was received and that consequently this country is at war with Germany."

"Hooray," yelled Robert. He was so glad. He liked nothing better than to see people shooting each other. And like most people in British Guiana, Robert was exceedingly patriotic, just mention England and he would "melt like butter."

Soon after war was declared a Portuguese man, who was a linesman on the railway, came into Robert's father's shop and started to rave on about Hitler and Mussolini. Robert's dad got up and hit him, then had him arrested for treason.

Posters inviting able bodied young men to fight for the honour of the motherland spread around town like wild fire.

One huge placard read: "Do you want to help the war cause? England needs you." This invitation caused a stir of excitement amongst young hungry men yearning adventure. The response was overwhelming. Each applicant had to sit a qualifying test — maths and dictation — and undergo a medical. Robert had heard that some of his friends had been turned away. But when the day came to sit the test, it was a mere formality.

When Robert landed in Scotland, his first inclination was to go back. He had left his hot part of the world, and now the lobes of his ears and his feet were burning from the cold.

The cultural differences also baffled him. Back in the West Indies anyone who did anything menial was black. From what Robert saw, the white people did not do much. They sat in offices and things like that. But on the train from Scotland to England, white women served biscuits and teas and Robert wondered why they were doing this. And all along the line he saw white women repairing the tracks. He had not expected to see white women with pick axes. Later he learned that women had been mobilised to help maintain the infrastructure while the men were away fighting.

Every night Robert dreamt of home, yet at daybreak he woke to the disappointment of England. But time was on his side. Within a year victory was theirs and it was time to go home.

One blustery autumn morning, Robert was all set to go back to British Guiana. He had accepted the British government's reluctant offer of a fare home. His bags were packed and the black cab was waiting. The taxi honked its horn, signalling the passenger to hurry up. Robert put his hand in his pocket and dragged out some shillings.

As he unpacked his suitcase, Robert decided it was

a question of ambition. What was he going back home for? From what he had heard the economic situation across the whole of the Caribbean had got worse. Thousands were without the means to earn a living. Only a handful prospered. He would go back when he had bettered himself, educationally and economically, and that time had not yet arrived.

CECIL'S STORY

Mrs C.E. Monroe of Coventry has returned home with her Jamaican husband after 14 months in the West Indies. 'I have come up against a great deal of prejudice from the other passengers, among whom are 60 Polish women. Many people have cut me off because they know my husband is coloured. He himself has been openly insulted.'
DAILY WORKER **JUNE 23 1948**

During the first week or so of the voyage, passing the time was easy. The Windrushians got on well and mainly congregated in the lounge relaxing on the floral armchairs playing dominoes, or just chatting and sipping rum that had been smuggled on board.

When T had gone to town to get his passport, he discovered that to go to England it was not enough to be a cultivator. To go to England, passengers had to have a profession or a trade. T said he was a carpenter.

At first he was nervous that he would have to compete for jobs with skilled craftsmen, but when the men got to know each other, although there were several professionals and ex-servicemen, most of those on board were like him: young hard working labourers who just wanted the opportunity to show what they could do.

"Me hear England is paved with gold. Me going to take some of that gold back home," T laughed.

It was night-time, the rays of the moon lit up the mauve ocean. T, Charlie, Joe, Cecil, George and a couple of the others huddled on the upper deck taking in some sea air. The Atlantic breeze was sometimes a little too cool, but the upper deck was less cramped than down below and it was also the best prescription to ward off the ever-present threat of sea sickness.

"Yeah, me hear that too," agreed Charlie, exhaling smoke from his roll-up.

"Yes if you work hard, you will get your just reward," laughed Cecil. "There are lots of jobs and opportunities, that's why I'm going back there."

Cecil Holness had been lured to England by the invitation to war through an advertisement in the Gleaner newspaper. It was only right that he should do his bit for the Mother country. He arrived in England four years earlier as ground crew in the Royal Air Force.

The United States of America had also put out a request for assistance in the conflict. But Cecil's loyalties were with England. As a teenager, he had been weaned on Shakespeare, Milton and Tennyson, and could name all the British monarchs and rulers since 1066. A friend had told him that he wanted to be an American. But Cecil wanted to be an Englishman, so gentlemanly. An Englishman never swore, gambled or did anything out of order, he thought.

The war also gave him something to do. There were no jobs in Jamaica, no matter how qualified the applicant was. A few years before coming to England Cecil sat a test for a job in a hotel. The manager told him he was the only one to get all the questions right. But Cecil did not get the job. The owner had had a friend whose son wanted the job.

After the hostilities ended Cecil had been granted sixty-one days leave. He had had a good time back home in Jamaica, visiting friends, spending time with family, going to the beach. His leave had even been extended while waiting on the Windrush to come from the Middle East.

The RAF men had travelled to Jamaica first class. Cecil had been waited on hand and foot. But for him, the Windrush was like going back to camp, they had to serve their own food (an uninspiring choice of plain potatoes, meat, vegetables sometimes livened up with pickles and peppers some of the men had carried with them), make their own beds and live in cramped, stifling third class conditions.

Although Cecil did not know much about civilian life, he tried to encourage the others to try their chances.

"If you work hard, England is a good place," he said.

"I'm going to live in a big house, work as a tailor and, in five years time, I'll go back home . . . No, me going get a nice little office job. Buy a house, then I'll send for Eileen and the children. I think England will be good for me. Me have this friend in Nottingham. He left Jamaica nearly five years now. I hear he doing well for himself. Marry a white woman and have a couple a children."

"What about the woman ah England, Cecil?" George winked and nudged T's arm.

"Some of them are very friendly, but some of them think they are something special. When I was based at a camp in West Ruislip, we used to go to these dances. The boys complained that the white girls would not dance with them.

"One night I watched this girl refuse all the boys a dance. When the next song started I went over and asked her for a dance. She said no sorry I'm sitting this one out. Then a white airman went and asked her to dance and she jumped up. When I ask this girl again, she refuses. So I said to her 'Excuse me, why do you come to these dances? I'll tell you why, and I'm just quoting what your boys say to us at the billet. Most of you girls come here to get a man to shag you after the dance. And being as you won't shag a black man, that's why you wouldn't dance with us.'

"The girl start to cry and left the dance. We never saw her again," Cecil laughed.

"So, what you saying, Cecil . . . the women in England are loose?"

"Me never say that," he chuckled.

'MUTINY' ON BOARD

Yes, we have read about the 400 Jamaicans who, I understand, are due to arrive on their own initiative. I hope that, whatever happens, it will not eventually be decided that they should be put into any of our Hostels.

We have had some experience of dealing with Jamaicans, and I cannot say that the experience we have had makes one anxious to extend it, for of all the differing types of people and nationalities who come to us the most provocative troublemakers have been the West Indians. If we are asked to house these people we should press for their being medically examined.
Letter to Ministry of Labour and National Service from National Service Hostels Corporation
16 JUNE 1948

"That noise it killing me, man. Me have a headache. Stop it nuh man."

A few men had brought some Jumbe drums on the ship. For the past few days they had lashed them rhythmically while others clapped and moved their bodies to the beat. It was their song of hope. Others took to singing, tap dancing and holding impromptu concerts and poetry recitals.

"Me tired ah this. It has to stop," shouted Fat Sam, a balding high-coloured Kingston man. He did not share their need for such activities and was trying to sleep off the effects of a heavy rum-drinking session the night before.

"Sam, just cool, man. You're too miserable."

"Cha, me tired and vex, man."

"Just hush up Sam," shouted one of the players as he continued to beat his drum.

Sam stumbled out of his hammock, grabbed one of the drums and threw it overboard. It plummeted heavily into the dark waters.

"What you have to do that for?"

Tricks, one of the drummers, edged boldly towards Sam. The two men eyed each other menacingly. For a brief moment the tension was on the verge of erupting into violence

"Look, me sorry man, but the noise just getting to me," Sam retreated apologetically.

Tricks and the other music men eventually saw the funny side of it. They had to. It was a long journey so it was pointless falling out over such trivial matters.

For British Guianan, Andre Shervington, these petty squabbles were nothing compared to what he had witnessed on the voyage from England to the Caribbean. Andre had fought in the war and had been chosen as one of the RAF representatives to escort servicemen back home to the Caribbean.

Just a few hours into that voyage, the men made it clear only two things mattered: gambling and drinking. The adrenaline was high, these soldiers had helped England win the war and they looked forward to returning home as war heroes, having done the Empire proud.

But this combination of alcohol, male ego and money proved costly. When an argument had broken out, fighting was deemed the only way forward. Many of the servicemen were returning home with war souvenirs, and it took only the slightest provocation for them to reach for their guns and bayonets.

By the time the Royal Navy responded to the distress call, fighting had spread to all corners of the boat. But soon enough, the war souvenirs were back in safe hands and peace was restored, and the ship resumed its course for the Caribbean.

Charlie slapped down a double eight on the wooden box. Frank responded sharply with an eight one. Charlie came back again with a one three. Frank paused, eyed his opponent then glanced nervously at his hand. Deadlock.

"Me can't play," he quietly conceded.

"Wha'? Me win again. Me is champion domino man. You can never trouble me." Charlie roared with laughter. "Hand over ya dollar."

"21, 14, 25, 1, 7, 12"

"House."

"No man, me can't lose. Me have no money left."

"Patrick, come lend me a couple ah dollar, pound, shilling, whatever. Dis time me feel lucky," the youngster rubbed his hard leathery hands with anticipation.

"Glenroy, you ah run outta luck and credit. Just hush up and let the rest of us play."

Faced with defeat, Glenroy slumped back in his chair and let the others play on.

"14, 8, 3, 5, 4,11"

"House."

"Me have one number to go until me win. Me losing money. You know how long this money tek to save. Me work hard for it. What me left with for Englan'? You sure this not a fix?"

"We nuh force you to play or spend yuh money."

Shortly after the captain banned gambling on the ship, too many men were losing the hard earned money that they had saved up to help them through the first few weeks in England.

WELCOME TO THE MOTHERLAND

Mr Holden warns me that 400 Jamaicans are landing at Tilbury on 19th June. The Colonial Office have appealed to the Ministry of Health who refuse to accommodate them.
COLONIAL OFFICE MEMORANDUM JUNE **1948**

The novelty of the great voyage soon wore off and the monotony set in. Every day it was the same ritual: rise early, have breakfast, walk, read, talk, have lunch, walk, read, talk, have dinner, talk, read, then go to bed. The days were long, but the nights were even longer.

The cramped sleeping conditions meant that one man's snoring could keep twenty men awake. Even so, T felt fortunate with his bunk bed. Others were not so lucky. Each night they searched for somewhere warm and sheltered to lay their head for the night.

The Windrushians had been sailing for twenty days. T diligently marked off each day in his note pad. "Not long to go now," he thought.

Some of the passengers told him that the harsher the weather got, the nearer they were to England. It

COLOURED FOLK GET A COLD WELCOME

HUNDREDS of West Indian immigrants to this country had a cold and unfriendly welcome as they arrived at Waterloo Station on Sunday evening.

Dressed in their cotton frocks and light suits, they left the station to be greeted by about 30 men carrying "Keep Britain White" banners.

Police tried to move the demonstrators on, as the new immigrants stood in Waterloo-rd. watching quietly, showing no emotion.

Altogether 750 immigrants arrived on Sunday.

No home

Yesterday some of the immigrants had already found their way to Brixton police station.

Some stopped to ask if the police knew of anywhere they could stay.

One couple told the station sergeant that they had some relatives " somewhere in London, and please could you help us find them."

The police told them they would have to make their own inquiries.

was now certainly much colder than T had ever experienced before. At night even though he went to bed covered from head to toe, he lay awake shivering. During the day he paced up and down the deck in a vain attempt to generate some heat.

The monotony of the voyage became more bearable with the thought that they were now in the final stretch of the journey. The Windrushians talked long into the night about what they would achieve in England. But now they were confidently reassured in the knowledge that these dreams were now closer to being realised.

As the Windrush neared England, some of the stowaways got anxious. During the passage, a handful had been caught and locked up in one of the cabins. But for the majority, blending in with the rest of the passengers had not been a problem, particularly when they were on their side. But now it was even more crucial that they were not found, they were too close to their destination to have it all taken away from them. If they were found they would be sent back home.

In the dead of night, before the Windrush was due to arrive at the docks, some of the stowaways put on their old clothes, secured their best suits on their backs, tied a rope around their waists and lowered themselves into the dark murky water.

The screams and cries rang through the deck. None of them had anticipated how cold the water would be. Those on board helped pluck the shivering men out of the sea.

"T, you'd better read this, man." Frank thrust a typed note into his hand then left T alone to digest its content:

I could not honestly paint you a very rosy picture of your future. Conditions in England are not as favourable as you may think.

Various reports you have heard about a shortage of labour are very misleading. The shortage is not general. Unless you are highly skilled, your chances of finding a job are none too good.

On the other hand if you are a serious-minded person and prepared to work hard in any location you could make your way.

It is left to you to win the respect of all you come across, not only win it but maintain it, and do your utmost to succeed.

Hard work is the order of the day in Britain and if you think you cannot pull your weight, you might as well decide to return to Jamaica, even if you have to swim the Atlantic.
No slackers will be tolerated.

Identical pieces of paper were being circulated around the boat. They were apparently from an African flight lieutenant who was with the Colonial Office Welfare Department.

Rumours quickly flew around that a British naval boat was on its way to turn the Windrush around and send it back to the West Indies. Others said that the newspapers in England called for the Jamaicans not to be allowed in the country. A couple of ex-RAF men who had been strategically posted outside the radio room overheard the British Broadcasting Corporation news bulletin that people in Britain did not want the boat to be allowed to dock in England.

The Motherland was rejecting them. The jubilation of the imminent arrival quickly turned to sadness. They were so near, but yet so far.

Some of the men called for protest but, on reflection, it was decided that that was not an appropriate response. Others sat with their hands in their heads and cried.

THE WELCOMING COMMITTEE

Just before dusk this ship with its 'cargo of faith in Britain' anchored in midstream off here. Aboard are the Jamaicans the Ministry of Labour knew nothing about until they had set sail.

The Jamaicans lined the decks and because no press men were allowed on board they shouted to me:

'We won't be disappointed in England. Nothing could be as bad as what we have left. We want to help England back on her feet again. We'll work as hard as anyone for you. Give us a chance. They wouldn't even let us work in Jamaica.'

DAILY MIRROR **22 JUNE 1948**

Seven o'clock in the morning, the Windrush was finally allowed to dock in Tilbury.

The Windrushians waved, clapped and cheered as a rather small, official looking party clamoured off a dingy and boarded the ship. They spoke to the captain and then to a couple of the passengers, then one of the men dressed in a pinstriped navy suit stepped forward and introduced himself as Mr Cummings from the

WAS IT REALLY NECESSA[RY]

Forced to emigrate from their homeland, these puzzled-loo[king] Jamaicans seeking work in Britain may well be asking th[em]selves: "Was my journey really necessary," [a]s they wa[ited]

FIVE HUNDRED PAIRS OF WILLING HANDS

The Jamaicans Land in Britain

From PETER FRYER

FIVE HUNDRED pairs of willing hands grasped the rails of the Empire Windrush as she came alongside the landing stage at Tilbury early yesterday morning.

On board were 500 Jamaicans, every one of whom was eager to work in Britain.

Before they could land they had to see Colonial Office and Ministry of Labour Officials, whose job was to sort them out according to experience and ability.

By a lucky chance a Colonial Office welfare man was on the ship during the voyage and he had been able to make a rough classification.

Colonial Office.

"First of all, let me welcome you to Great Britain and express hope that you all achieve the objectives which have brought you here.

"I know that many of you have been in this country before, but to those of you who are new to England, and who will be particularly in need of guidance, I want to say that I hope you especially will take very careful heed of the advice which is given to you.

"Tomorrow morning representatives of the Ministry of Labour and National Service will board this ship in order to give what assistance they can.

"Now I come to the advice and help which I think we as officials can give you. We have asked that you should be separated into three categories . . . "

The pale Englishman went on to say that those who intended to volunteer for the armed forces would be given temporary accommodation at the Colonial Servicemen's Club in central London, at their own expense. Those who had friends to go to would be given free travel warrants from Tilbury to their places of destination.

Then the Englishman came to the category that concerned T and most of the others.

"I now want to address my friends who may have nowhere to go and no plans whatsoever . . . I am afraid that you will have many difficulties . . . "

It was curiously touching to walk along the landing-stage in the grey light of the early morning and see against the white walls of the ship rows upon rows of dark pensive faces looking down upon England, most of them for the first time. Had they thought England a golden land in a golden age? Some had, with their quaint amalgam of American optimism and African innocence.

MANCHESTER GUARDIAN JUNE 23 1948

Grey and white speckled sea gulls flew around the harbour as the Windrushians took their first uncertain but proud steps off the ship. T was bewildered by his strange new surroundings.

At the end of the quayside, a small dignified looking welcoming committee consisting of a few armed forces representatives, Colonial Office officials with their bowler hats and policemen efficiently ushered the new arrivals to the relevant sections. The proceedings were overlooked by a handful of journalists.

"Well me is here," T muttered contemplating the new chapter of his life that was just about to begin.

STREETS PAVED WITH MOULD

Some of the 492 Jamaican emigrants who arrived
in Britain yesterday in the Empire Windrush wore
expensive suits.

There were even emigrants wearing zoot-style
suits — very long-waisted jackets, big padded
shoulders, slit pockets and peg-top trousers —
costing 15 to 28 pounds. There were flash ties
(from 10s 6d to one pound 1s) and white-and-tan
shoes (75s). The explanation was given last night
by one quietly dressed Jamaican, Oswald
Denniston, 35, sign-painter.

Mr Denniston told me: 'Most of us are job-
seekers but others are here to finish their trades
and education. The very poor can't leave Jamaica.
They must have 28 pounds for their passage and
another five pounds when they sail.'
DAILY MIRROR WEDNESDAY 23 JUNE 1948

The bus pulled slowly out of Tilbury Docks heading
west towards London taking the new arrivals to an
unknown destination.

The Windrushians were captivated, but

disappointed by their new surroundings. Everything was bleak. Colours merged as if a greyish-green rinse had been stroked across the Kent landscape, and a damp misty cloud enveloped the atmosphere. The buoyant colours of the Caribbean were a distant memory.

Within the hour, as the vehicle neared central London, the long winding country stretches fringed with bushes were transformed into identical streets lined with shabby, run-down three-storey houses stacked side by side. The pace of the bus slowed as other vehicles took to the road.

A crowd of rather woeful-looking men with flat caps and women armed with baskets of shopping scurried along the narrow footpaths, skilfully dodging grubby carefree children playing hopscotch on the pavements. The Windrushians waved cheerily at the white passers-by. But soon became mystified by the perplexed, even horrified reactions.

Then all of a sudden the bus came to a halt.

"Here we are, Clapham Deep Shelter," shouted a voice from the front of the coach. "This is where you get off."

The deep shelter had been opened during the war as emergency housing in the event of a German bomb attack. The escort ushered the Windrushians to make their way through the tent-like opening, then slid open heavy wooden doors bearing a huge no smoking sign, and beckoned them to step inside.

Nervously, the men piled in this cumbersome

elevator and were transported one hundred and fifty feet below, deep into the bowels of the busy south London town. They curiously eyed the network of poorly lit, clammy, musty tunnels that had been offered to them as residence. It was primitive and unwelcoming, like a sparsely furnished rabbit's warren. But in a strange new land, there were few alternatives.

Each man was allocated a place at one of the endless rows of bunk beds and given coarse white linen and a grey blanket to sleep under. The weary Windrushians slept, dreaming of a prosperous future in this new land.

The chill that crept through the tunnels prematurely woke men who had been accustomed to rising to the warmth of the sunlight.

After being served with a cheery cup of traditional English tea and coarse white bread with dripping — which they were warned to be grateful for as post-war Britain still had strict rationing — the men were strongly advised to try their luck and venture into the outside world.

Forty Jamaicans, who came to Britain on the Empire Windrush, are now staying in the Clapham Common deep shelters, were given a public welcome to Lambeth at Brixton Astoria on Wednesday by the Mayor.

Many of them were law students, dockers, potential chemists and scientists who had left their homeland because of the difficulties of finding work there.

One man was Norman Hamilton, a 24-year-old ex-RAF wireless operator who served in the forces in Britain during the war. He comes from the capital Kingston.

He said, 'I visited London many times when I was here last, I like the city a lot. We were completely disillusioned when we were demobbed in Jamaica after being assured that jobs would be awaiting us. There was nothing at all. We all look to Britain for a brighter future.'

At the Brixton Astoria to greet them was Lt. Col. Marcus Lipton, Brixton MP. Col Lipton, who had stated in the House of Commons a few hours previously that south Londoners would make them welcome, repeated the pledge and urged them to regard themselves as honoured guests:

'We want you to regard this country as your second home. I hope it will not be very long before each of you is provided for in a dignified fashion.'
SOUTH LONDON PRESS 25 JUNE 1948

Things had been hard back home in Jamaica, but T was not prepared for the poverty and squalor in England. The buildings were tiny and neglected. On almost ever corner, grimy kids played amongst broken glass and bricks.

"Hey Nigger, Nigger," they shouted.

The insults he received from the children were matched by the hostility from adults. People on the street went all out to avoid his path. But their coldness fitted in with the bleak, grey surroundings. He could sense he was an unwanted outsider.

T and the others had been steered to a Labour Exchange just a few miles away in Brixton to register for work.

Inside, a handful of white men sat idly waiting to be summoned by the anonymous men and women who sat behind the long wooden counter. Peeping from under the flat caps and trilbies that partially concealed their faces, they eyed the black job seekers with immense suspicion.

After undergoing a rigorous interrogation about their skills and aptitude, some of the Windrushians were handed small white cards with details of where they should report for work. Others were told to come back tomorrow, maybe they would have something for them then.

The next day and the day after that were the same. Each morning the Windrushians went to the Labour Exchange, explored the surrounding area, then went back to the Shelter to play cards or read. For those, like T, who had not yet found work, money was fast running out. The Colonial Office decided to publicise their plight in local newspapers.

Then T had a lucky break. The owner of a factory in Derby had spotted this advertisement for "cheap labour" and came to the Shelter looking for workers. He had taken on thirty-five willing hands and with no delay the men gathered together their humble belongings and caught the next northbound train.

The Men from Jamaica Are Settling Down

'YOU COULDN'T MEET A NICER CROWD'

From PETER FRYER

THE large marquee near Clapham deep shelter was taken down yesterday. The people of Clapham will miss the colourful ties and cheerful smiles of their Jamaican guests.

The group of immigrants has been steadily dwindling as more and more left to take up jobs and go into private lodgings.

Of the 500 who came across in the Empire Windrush three weeks ago, 240 placed themselves in the hands of the Colonial Office. All but 30 of these have been found work.

These have gone to a hostel at Peckham, and they, too, will soon start work.

How are the Jamaicans settling down? That was the question I set out yesterday to answer, in conversation with the men themselves and with those who have come into contact with them.

First, the testimony of a Ministry of Labour official in charge of a large number of hostels in Onslow Square, South Kensington—a man who works amid a babel of tongues belonging to a dozen different nationalities.

"You couldn't wish to meet a nicer crowd," he told me, "They are cheerful and willing, and we have had no trouble of any kind, nor do we expect any."

A moment later he added reflectively: "Of course, I'm against all this colour bar. I've travelled about the world too much for that . . ."

Refused Rooms

Some of the Jamaicans have, it is true, come up against colour prejudice—from a café proprietor

Easy Money

The Clapham Deep Shelter was finally evacuated of Jamaican workers on Monday 12 July, i.e. less than three weeks after their arrival. It is interesting to note that the Manager and Staff of the Shelter spoke well of the men's behaviour and no incident of disorder or even minor loss of belongings was reported during the occupation period.
EMPIRE WINDRUSH — FINAL REPORT, COLONIAL OFFICE
22 JULY 1948

Rusty barbed wire strangled the peaks of the high-rise brick wall that encircled the immense concrete building. The shavings of paint peeling off the tired structure and weeds that blossomed in the path way bore testimony to many years of neglect.

Its inhabitants — frail looking Europeans with sullen eyes — wandered the parameters. The war was now over and these prisoners of the conflict were free to go, but circumstance had cruelly dealt a further sentence. They had nowhere to go.

This was the old prisoner of war camp in Castle

Donington, the new home of the Windrushians who had been offered work in the northern town of Derby.

The living quarters consisted of row after row of identical basic metal beds covered with thin shabby mattresses and off-white sheets.

Each morning the Windrushians rose to the call of toast and eggs frying in wedges of lard, waiting to be washed down with a mug of weak tea. To the Caribbean palate, the diet was almost nauseating, but they woke hungry and hurriedly ate dreaming of sugary cornmeal, fresh bread with guava jelly or saltfish and fried dumplings.

Then at eight-thirty like clockwork, a bus transported them to their place of employment fifteen miles away.

Stanton Iron Works was an antiquated remnant of the industrial revolution. On the men's first day of work, they had to report to the doctor. Once behind the makeshift screen, they were told to strip while being observed under close scrutiny, then had their heads searched for lice. The cold intrusive hands were unpleasant and demeaning, but the Windrushians reluctantly agreed to it. It was their passport to work.

The first few weeks at Stanton Iron Works, the Windrushians were not allowed to work inside the factory. They would punch their clocking in cards at nine in the morning, then spend the rest of the day milling around and playing cards until it was time to clock off. Some of the men made up some weights from scrap pieces of iron and passed the time exercising.

"Me never know this is what working in England would be like. It don't make sense him paying us to sit around," T said. Back home, he had worked so hard in any job he was given. This treatment devalued his good intentions.

"Well, me nuh complain. Nine pound to sit around at our leisure, okay with me," laughed Charlie sealing down a fresh roll-up.

The tedium was momentarily broken by the satisfaction of the first pay day. Friday at four-thirty they stood in line to be handed a brown envelope.

"What? Me thought it was nine pound me getting?" boomed T looking down at the contents of his pay packet.

"It is, but they take off one pound tax and one-fifteen for digs. What's left? Nothing for we to save," one of the other sighed.

T took the wages, stuffed a pound in an envelope to send back to his mother, and planned to put the rest in the jar under his mattress. This was his going home money.

This routine went on for weeks. They clocked in, sat around, smoked, talked, made tea, and clocked off in the evening. Then suddenly, one by one they were all put to work. If they could call it that.

T might be asked to move a table for the day or a lamp. That was all. It was as if they were not to be trusted. And none of the white workers spoke to the new black arrivals. They simply eyed them with suspicion.

T had expected to be wearing a suit to a job in an office somewhere, not overalls in a factory. He wrote his mother regular letters and always enclosed a pound note. He knew she would be disappointed to hear that England was not the place they had thought it would be, so he carefully crafted letters that would not belie his disappointment.

The admittedly limited experience of the Ministry of Agriculture is that Jamaicans are not suitable for farm work in this country. For example, a number who offered themselves for agriculture from the Empire Windrush were in practice useless and unwilling, and all of them left agriculture in a short space of time.

If the Ministry of Labour is able to find vacancies for them, there could be no possible objection ...should it be decided that it is politically essential that some West Indians, even if only in 'token' numbers, should be found jobs in this country.

WORKING PARTY OF THE EMPLOYMENT IN THE UNITED KINGDOM OF SURPLUS COLONIAL LABOUR OCTOBER 1948

NO BLACKS, NO IRISH, NO DOGS

It is difficult to get an accurate picture of how West Indian workers stand up to their jobs. It is perhaps a fair observation to say that there is a fair amount of movement from job to job. The arrival of the Empire Windrush men and the placing of them in employment has been a recent experience.

On the whole, it would appear that the men have remained in the employment found for them, with the exception of a small group placed in a tin-plate works in Wales. These men complained that the work was unsuitable and that they could not work near the furnaces. The result is that they drifted to Cardiff where the majority are unemployed.

On the other hand, a large group sent to Bicester (the Royal Ordnance depot) have settled down reasonably well. A small group employed as radio technical trainees in Wales are well reported on. The Salvation Army are satisfied with the dozen tailors whom they employed.

In London, it has been observed that, on the whole, the men have kept their jobs, e.g: some 12-18 at the General Electric Company Ltd, north

Wembley and also another 20 in temporary Government service.

WORKING PARTY ON THE EMPLOYMENT IN THE UNITED KINGDOM OF SURPLUS COLONIAL LABOUR OCTOBER 1948

The leaves on the trees turned from green to yellow to brown, then they fell. At the same time, the gentle summer breeze graduated into a chilly wind. In preparation, T had spent almost two weeks wages buying scarves, pullovers, gloves, hats and coats to protect himself from the intrusive chill. When he returned home from work, he battled with the other Jamaicans for a place near the small fire to thaw his numb body.

He stayed at Castle Donington for six months, now it was time to move on. Around town he saw adverts for rooms to rent, but when he went to inquire it was always the same old story:

"No Irish, no dogs, no coloureds."

T had been offered a room. But when he ventured inside, the sheets of the bed were dirty and the mattress mouldy. The stale stench of urine had made his stomach churn. Three pounds a week, he would have had to have been a fool to take it.

"Sorry, my wife just let the room," said one man, hurriedly closing the front door. But others were not so polite.

"We don't want your sort around here. People don't take much to coloured folk," a woman shrieked from an upstairs window, threatening to pour a bowl of dirty water if he did not "clear off". T had lost count of the times that doors had been slammed in his face.

Then a fellow Jamaican had offered him a space in a damp six-room house with no hot water in Derby with ten others. Eighteen shillings a week. T took it.

None of the men in the house cooked. That was the way most of them had been brought up. Mothers, sisters or maids had taken care of all the meals. The men had a saying, "Fire never made in this house until weekend." They had befriended some women who they could depend on to cook a decent hot meal when they came over to visit.

Though he appreciated this gesture, T missed home cooking. They did not have much, but Sunday nights his mother would cook rice and peas — that was his favourite. It made a change from the yam, banana and breadfruit picked from the back yard, that they had during the week.

"T, me hear there's a dance hall on Langley Road. Not too expensive. We should go there, show them white people how to do the jive." Egbert leaped up and started to shuffle around the room.

"Wha', Egbert you need to learn some new moves. Where you learn to jive like that?" Laughed Joseph nimbly be-bopping in front of the fire.

The men had spent most of their weekends at the local pub. They would have a drink, some stout or whiskey then come home. Nothing too exciting but it broke the monotony of the day. The strangest thing was getting used to seeing women drinking alongside men. Back home no woman ever dared to go into the roadside rum shops.

That Saturday, T put on his blue pinstriped pants, matching jacket and burgundy tie. His freshly waxed hair had a sharp parting in it. He looked good.

The suit he had really wanted to wear was lost. He had sent it to the laundry and when he went to pick it up, they could not find it. "Lie them ah tell," thought T.

They mocked the way the English dressed — it was so old fashioned. The English were still wearing wide-legged trousers and short jackets — but the Jamaicans had straight trousers imported to the island from the United States. The style-conscious among them wanted to know where they bought it and how they made it. T went to the tailor and gave him exact instructions. The tailors tried their best, but the English, though they had nice cloth, could not compete with the Americans.

It was the same with cars. T was surprised to find England's roads and vehicles not that dissimilar to Jamaica. He had expected flash, revolutionary models. But instead found bicycles and trams. Any man who *did* have a car was a very rich man indeed — and even then it was an outdated model.

"You people are not allowed in this dance hall. We have standards to uphold." An elderly white man dressed in a suit used his body to block the doorway to the Mecca dance hall.

T, Egbert, Hollis and Thomas edged forward.

"Why, we have money, if that's what you are worried about."

"We don't need your money. Now please." The doorman gestured for the men to move to make way for the regular clientele. Aware that a crowd of curious young men and women had gathered round, the tone of his voice raised.

"Now are you lot going to move? Or do we have to move you?"

It would have been easy to make more of the matter. Smash a few bottles, fight, create a scene. But the Windrushians left quietly, with their dignity intact.

For the next few Saturdays T and the others went to the dance hall and tried to reason with the manager to let them in. Eventually they were allowed into a separate room away from the main area, where they could hear the music.

Jamaican George Powe was in the neighbouring town of Nottingham. He was faced with a similar colour bar. But his solution was different. When the landlord in the Acorn pub had refused to serve him and a West African friend, arguing that they would "bring prostitutes into the pub", George jumped behind the bar and served himself.

It was a last resort. He found many of the dance halls and public houses were closed to West Indians. Sometimes they were allowed in the public bar, not

A bitter cry from a Jamaican in the Midland

I protest against the colour bar

by HORACE HALLIBURTON

FOR the past eight months — since I arrived in Birmingham in search of a job — I have lived in the Causeway Green Hostel where the recent racial disturbances have occurred.

The problem of Causeway Green is by no means unique in this country. It is an example of Great Britain's colour - bar. Similar instances are constantly arising in other parts of the country.

My 80 fellow West Indians in the hostel know only too well that the ill-feeling and fighting of the past week cannot be

Mr. Halliburton, 24 years old, is the son of a Kingston, Jamaica, sugar overseer. He was educated at Calabar High School where he passed the Cambridge School Certificate examination and earned exemption from Matriculation on the results. From 1941 until 1944 he worked in the administrative section of the Public Works Department in Jamaica and at the age of 19 emigrated to the United States. For several months he worked in American factories but went home in 1945 to resume employment in the engineering section of the Public Works Department. He came to this country in May of last year, spent six weeks in London, fire

administrative work in engineering. As a vocation I trained myself to become a skilled metal turner, but I can name 12 firms whom I have visited for the purpose of finding employment.

The only work that Great Britain can offer me is navvying — or swopping the roads. I am not afraid to tackle either, but I have tried to make something of my life and I do not think it is fair to expect me to settle to work with no prospects and no future. Would you do it — or would you go on looking for the job you are qualified to undertake?

Many of my countrymen have already given up all hope of finding this and are doing unskilled jobs to save up the passage money to go back home.

They write letters home full of despondency, and so the

good enough for the lounge.

He had seen an article in *The Times* newspaper some years before. The West Indian cricketer, Learie Constantine, had won a case regarding a colour bar at a hotel in London.

Despite coming to England to fight in the war, George had never cared much for the country. Growing up he had never seen many white people. His community was very anti-white and there was never any intention that they should mix with white people. George had not accepted the way white people had treated black people historically. He remembered reading an article entitled, "Now we know", in the *Gleaner* by the celebrated Caribbean writer Roger Mais.

It urged Jamaicans not to fight for the imperialist ruler. Quoting the experiences of Emperor Haile Selassie and the Italian intervention in Africa, Mais warned that "atrocities were being committed against our people." He was swiftly arrested and charged with treason and sedition.

But although he shared this sentiment, the sway of adventure was too much, George wanted to join his high school friends and fight in the armed forces.

George Powe moved from city to city in search of work. After a brief spell in Liverpool, then in Birmingham, eventually he was employed at a Nottingham firm, Dowshall Illumination Engineers, as an electrical fitter.

Each day, a young white woman would come in and try to spark up a conversation with George. Sometimes she would bring a few sandwiches and a flask of tea. George told her not to, experience had told him that it could only lead to trouble.

A few weeks before, he had gone for an engineering job in Aston. The director invited him into his office. "Anything to drink?" he asked.

"I don't mind if I have a coffee," replied George.

He poured himself a drink and got one of his staff to make George the coffee.

"I'll get the job, no problem," thought George confidently.

After about an hour, the director said: "Mr Powe you're a very intelligent man, but I'm afraid I can't employ you."

"Why?" asked George.

"Because white women are employed here and if we should employ you, you'll have to move around with the women and the other workers won't like it."

He then offered George five pounds for his time. It was a lot of money, but George refused and told him to "f*** off."

"Mr Dowshall wants to see you in his office, straight away."

"What have I done now?' George asked himself. "My work's good, I'm always punctual, polite."

"Sit down George," the boss said as George entered his office.

"George, my boy, you're going to have to leave. The men don't like you speaking to the white women."

The way it was said, George knew it was not worth putting up a fight. The decision had been made.

WHITE GIRLS OBJECTED

Colour divides city hosiery workers

ENGLISH girls at a Nottingham textile factory are refusing to work with coloured girls. So the management have decided on a policy of segregation.

The production manager of the firm said last night that the segregation decision was taken as the only possible solution to a problem that is causing headaches in local hosiery circles—the shortage of machinists.

In an effort to combat this shortage, he continued, his firm engaged coloured girl machinists. Their work, although slow, was satisfactory on cheaper classes of goods.

Notices started

Mon: African and West Indian girls were employed—and then white girls started asking for transfers to other departments, or gave notice.

"There was a most definite feeling against the c o l o n i a l worker," declared the production manager.

A big problem faced the firm: they either lost their experienced white girls, or ceased to employ coloured girls. Either decision would result in a return to their primary problem of labour shortage.

On cheap work

" Our coloured girls now work on cheap goods under one white supervisor in their own department.

"Ultimately, we hope to replace her with a coloured supervisor," explained the executive, "preferably a girl with a keen sense of discipline."

Initially, the coloured girls are paid between £4 and £5 a week. Expert machinists can command wages of £12 to £14 a week.

Mr. John Burghart, secretary of the Nottingham branch of the

He was given two weeks notice.

George could not go back to Jamaica, even though he so desperately wanted to. He was now a known left-wing agitator, a communist. He had joined the Communist Party in Nottingham. A Home Office stamp in his passport stated that he could not go to an independent Commonwealth country. They had accused him of not liking white people, which was not true. It was the injustice they imposed on the West Indians that he hated.

For several years now he had witnessed at first hand, the treatment meted out to the West Indian immigrants. The racism, the injustice, the humiliation. Black people sometimes worked one hundred hours a week and were getting paid much less than their white colleagues who were working forty hours. Through the Communist movement he had found sympathetic white people to help fight the cause. He believed change could come through the Communist Party.

St William Grant had been a guiding force throughout George's life. Back home in Jamaica, St William had held meetings in Victoria Park, Kingston. Though he was illiterate, he was such a powerful speaker on the subject of the disadvantages faced by black people. The memory of his words motivated George to improve the situation of his people and help get rid of colonialism and gain independence for Jamaica, the

GAMING HOUSE IN CAFE YARD

POLICE RAID DICE PARTY

A 19-YEAR-OLD coloured girl was at West London on Friday fined £25 and ordered to pay £10 10s. costs after police officers had described a raid on an outhouse in the back yard of a Notting Hill cafe where coloured men were gambling with dice and cards.

Thelma Williams, a factory hand, of St. Anns Road, Notting Hill, was convicted of having the care of a common gaming house at premises in Blenheim Crescent, Notting Hill.

Together with nine coloured men, the girl was also bound over not to frequent gaming houses for a year on a charge of being found on premises alleged to be a common gaming house.

P.C. Leslie Marshall said he saw a number of coloured men go out through the cafe kitchen door into an outhouse in the yard where they began to play dice round a table. Later there were 20 coloured men present and a pack of cards was produced. The coloured girl paid several visits to the outhouse. There was a sudden crash of glass and several of the men ran out and climbed over a wall.

DOOR FORCED

P.C. Alan Grant, who took part in the police raid, said he had to force the cafe door. He overtook the girl who was shouting in agitated tones. He then forced the kitchen door to get into the yard. He found 10 coloured men in the outhouse in which there was a table covered with a grey blanket. He found a black dice.

Chief Supt. Frederick Fieldsend said the girl told him : " No-one is in charge of the premises. I just look after them for my brother." Told the police were satisfied she was responsible for allowing gaming, the girl replied : " I know it goes on. I told them the law would come sooner or later."

Pleading not guilty, the girl denied knowing gaming was taking place in the outhouse. She added that it was her brother's cafe and on this evening he had gone out for a short time.

Mr. R. G. Mays, prosecuting, described the premises as being " of bad repute." He added that the gaming was on a fair scale because the 10 arrested coloured men had nearly £140 between them when arrested. One man had £95 of it which suggested he had either done very well or had been the banker.

NINE ARRESTS

The nine coloured men who admitted being frequenters were :— Charles Edghill, 23, student, of Tunstall Road, Brixton ; George Webb, 31, labourer, of Bramley Road, Notting Hill ; Nathan Rainford, 23, labourer, of Moorhouse Road, Notting Hill ; Wilburt Campbell, 27, disc jockey, of Silchester Road, Notting Hill ; Nicholas McKoy 31, painter, of Franconia Road, Clapham ; Vincent Brown, 28, unemployed, of Westbourne Park Road, Notting Hill ; Eric Bernard Dawson, 29, carpenter, of Bramley Road, Notting Hill ; Francis Johnson, 23, waiter, of Tavistock Road, Paddington, Frederick Mowatt, barber, of Rochester Road, Camden Town. Lewis Jones, 22, unemployed, of St. Anns Road, Notting Hill, did not appear.

island he so dearly loved.

It was quite natural that George became a political agitator, writing letters to Members of Parliament. There was so much that he felt angry about. He joined the Colonial Freedom Movement and the Committee of African Organisations. He even helped set up the Youth Freedom Movement which fought to rid Jamaica of colonialism.

SWEETHEARTS

If, in order to deal with an unwanted influx of Jamaicans, we institute controls which will affect the traditional freedom of movement from all Commonwealth countries into the United Kingdom, we shall be subject to strong political criticism both in this country and in other Commonwealth countries. The existing freedom of movement is of great political importance and is a matter to which people in, say, Australia and New Zealand attach great importance.
LETTER FROM SECRETARY OF STATE FOR COMMONWEALTH RELATIONS TO HOME OFFICE **1954**

There was a gentle knock at the front door.

"Who can that be at this time of the night?" wondered T Cooper as he reluctantly got up from his chair . He was relaxing with a cup of sweet tea and his newspaper before it was time to go on the night shift.

"Surprise, surprise." Enid stood in the doorway beaming. "What? You paralysed or something? Give me a hug."

"Enid? Wha' . . . What are you doing here?" T

stammered in shock.

He put his arms around the young woman, picked up her suitcase and steered her inside.

"How you find me?" He was puzzled.

"It was easy man, me have your address." Smiled the pretty Jamaican woman standing before him.

T had known Enid since they were children. As far back as he could remember T had loved her, he knew she was the right girl for him. It had been painful leaving her behind in Jamaica, but T knew that if he was ever going to have anything to offer Enid, it was a decision *he* had to make. And besides, when he left Jamaica, T was not yet ready for the commitment of marriage.

But now things were different. T had been prudent and thrifty during the first year in England. After moving from place to place, he had finally saved enough money to put down a deposit on a house. He found a three-bedroom terrace for one thousand five hundred pounds. It was sparsely decorated and in need of repair, but it was his own home.

Enid was a good girl from a respectable home. She was very popular back home, not the sort of girl who went to dance halls or hung around with boys. So finally T decided to "make she come".

The couple had made meticulous, long distance arrangements for Enid's arrival. T wrote lengthy letters to her parents reassured them that their daughter would be well looked after, while Enid carefully wrapped and packaged items that T said she might need for her new life in England.

Days before Enid's arrival T swept, mopped, polished throughout the house, then started all over again. Everything had to be just right.

On the day that Enid was due to arrive, T had made the long journey to Southampton. As scores of excited West Indians clamoured off the landing stage heading towards the London-bound boat train, T's eyes darted around furiously looking for Enid.

In the thick of the crowd, a young woman dressed in a yellow dress with a matching jacket was bending down, impatiently tightening the strap around her suitcase.

She was the right complexion, the right build, even her dress looked familiar.

"Enid," T shouted. "Over here."

The woman looked up and glared at T curiously. It was not her.

As the herds of passengers filtering off the ship slowed into a trickle, T became anxious. In his head he read and re-read the letter Enid had sent him, there was no way he could have got the days muddled.

T waited and waited until the last few passengers scrambled off the landing stage. Enid was not on the ship. Maybe she had changed her mind.

"Me missed the boat, so me tek another one."

"But how you get to me house?"

"When me arrive in London, me stop at a friend. She put me on a train to Derby, then me tek a cab."

It was the best news he had received in a long

while. But that evening, T still went to work.

A deputation from Birmingham City Council are likely to ask to see the Colonial Secretary soon about West Indian immigration. They will tell him that by their policy of 'deliberate laissez faire', which is said to show itself in a complete absence of control over Jamaican labour, his department are evading their obligations at the cost of creating unbearable problems for local authorities.

There is a scarcity of labour in Birmingham itself that hardly anybody, irrespective of colour or creed, could fail to find work if he is able-bodied and willing. But once here the Jamaicans have to be housed, and Birmingham already has a waiting list of more than 50,000 white would-be tenants. The Jamaicans are therefore overcrowding an already overcrowded city.
THE TIMES 22 OCTOBER 1954

Enid became Mrs Timothy Cooper about six months after she arrived from Jamaica. It was a small, simple affair, as the newly-weds did not know that many people in England to invite. The only woman they knew was Enid's bridesmaid.

After the service the wedding party bought some drinks, cooked some food and had a meal at home. The cake was parceled up and sent back home to their family and friends.

NORMAN'S STORY

In October 1948 the *Orbita* brought 180 West Indians to Liverpool, and three months later 39 Jamaicans, 15 of them women, arrived at Liverpool in the *Reina del Pacifico*. Next summer the *Georgic* brought 253 West Indians to Britain, 45 of them women. A few hundred came in 1950, about 1,000 in 1951, about 2,000 in 1952 and again in 1953. Larger numbers arrived in the next four years, including many wives and children of men who had settled here: 24,000 in 1954; 26,000 in 1956; 22,000 in 1957; 16,000 in 1958. Ten years after the *Empire Windrush* about 125,000 West Indians had come over since the end of the war.

PETER FRYER, *STAYING POWER* 1984

19-year-old Norman Phillips clasped the railings and looked back at the isle of Trinidad and Tobago. He was almost tempted to jump off and swim back.

But then he remembered why he was going. He had to go. There was no work at home. No real industry had been developed on the island. There were the odd

jobs on the cotton or cocoa plantations. But a dollar a
day did not go far. And the work was hard. In the
country, silhouettes of women, men and children
dotted the landscape. Their hands bled from the
prickly leaves that encased the ripe cotton and their
backs ached from bending down to pick the buds from
the waist-high bushes.

For the higher paid jobs, your mother had to be
"carrying on" with the boss. Take Robert Martin. He
had grown up in the same neighbourhood as Norman.
They had both been brought up by their single parent
mothers, gone to the same schools, played together,
but that was where their paths separated.

When he was sixteen, Robert got a well paid job at
the bank as a clerk. It was soon after he started that
all the gossip began.

Robert's mother was an attractive woman. Late
forties, curves in the right places, smooth buttermilk
skin. Mr Jacobs the bank manager and Robert's
mother were "carrying on".

"Good luck to him," thought Norman.

Like Norman's mother, there were many young women
who were forced to bring their children up single-
handedly. Carnival time was a time when parents
feared for their young daughters the most.

The preparations would go on all year round. The
Mass players painstakingly stitched, wove and spun
feathers and gold bands into their creative costumes
while the steel bands would endlessly harmonise in
the pan yards.

Norman's mother had always tried to warn him to stay away from becoming too involved with Carnival. Like other parents, she frowned on young people "liming" or hanging about the pan yards where the players honed their beautiful melodies. But for Norman the call of the steel drum was too infectious.

Then at carnival itself, at five o'clock on J'ouvert morning, thousands would take to the streets and jump up with the bands to celebrate freedom from the Spanish, English and French colonial rulers.

But this time of physical over-indulgence extended to the sexual variety. Nine months after carnival, the birth rate would rocket. These children were dubbed carnival babies.

It was hard for the young girls because they were having children and their boyfriends had no jobs. They had to do what they could to make ends meet.

Norman's mother did not earn enough to provide for him and his sister, so he strayed. Norman left home and started to steal to survive. Coffee and cocoa were the most lucrative products sold on the black market. He would jump on the trains transporting the produce from the country then throw bags off on to the ground. Norman could get a good price from the sailors wanting to ship the products abroad.

For several months he could have a lucky run and not get caught. Other times they would catch him straight away. For several years he was in and out of borstals and prisons. It never worried him though, it was his trade.

At any one time, between five hundred and six hundred young people filled the borstal. Some were orphans or children whose parents could not look after them. Others were juvenile tearaways who were being taught a lesson.

So as not to be a burden on the Government, the young people were not only given a standard education, but also provided with tools to grow their own food and make their own prison clothes. But hundreds of teenagers locked up against their will provided a predictable recipe for trouble. Fights, theft and abuse were the order of the day.

Norman always fared well when he was inside. There were always a couple of his friends already locked up who would make sure he got a good job in the kitchen or bakery.

One day Norman sat on the stone bed in a dark, dirty cell with only a tiny window high up in the wall letting a few rays of light come in. The cell stunk of stale urine, and flies and cockroaches festered on scraps of food strewn on the floor, while thumb-sized mosquitoes feasted on his skin.

He was doing a six month stretch in the local jail for grievous bodily harm. A local boy had been harassing his girlfriend, Daphne, and the boy had to be taught a lesson.

Norman was used to men paying too much attention to his "brown-skinned gal". He thought so much of her that he had even added her name to Barbara's, Jean's, and the rest of the long list of young women tattooed on his torso. But this admirer had gone too far forcing Norman to slash his face with a knife.

"I've had enough of this place. The next thing is that they're going to hang us. Let's jump a ship and ride, because there is nothing here," he anguished, burying his head deep in the soiled mattress.

"But Norman, where we going go?" Norman shared the cell with his friend Ernest.

"Let's go to England. Me hear people so rich there," suggested Norman.

He had always seen himself as a "lucky fella". When he came out of prison, he was to wait for his mate to finish his nine-month stretch, but ran into an old friend, Rudy, who said his sister was going to England and that he was thinking of stowing away. Rudy had a pass to go on board to see her off and they decided to go and get another for Norman and they would stowaway together.

Hundreds of people dressed in Sunday bests, carrying suitcases and carefully wrapped packages queued to get on the ship.

"Please carry with care: Mr Winston Green, 116 Firs Lane, Brixton, London, Care Of Mrs Enid Blake, The Lawns, Bridgehope, Durham." the scrawled inscriptions on the luggage read.

Norman dressed up in the best clothes he had, the only clothes he had — yellow suit with a mustard tie and butter-coloured shoes and a few dollars in his pocket. "I feel good, man," he thought.

There was so much bustle and confusion, as passengers clamoured on board weighted down with their luggage, that it was easy for Norman to stay on the boat and blend in with the passengers.

"Norman, they catch Joe, you know." Rudy came bursting into the bar where his friend was relaxing with a tipple of rum and a cigarette.

"What? Where they catch him?" Norman was surprised, "Fast Joe" as he had been known was a slippery fellow, always able to manoeuvre himself out of trouble.

"He fell asleep in the bar last night, after we had those few drink. One of the crew was going round with a torch. Me hear they take him to the Captain and lock him in a cabin with a few others who they catch."

"Boy, we tell him to be careful. Well we not going to get caught. We too smart for that," boasted Norman. "Listen, here's what we going to do."

Each night the pair slept in different cabins. So that the other passengers did not get suspicious, they only spent a short time in each one. But keeping clean was a problem. With just one set of clothes, they unsuccessfully attempted to wash out their shirts, vest and underpants in the sink. But after a week they decided it would be best if they did not hang around people too much.

At meal time, they went around the boat taking the meal tickets of the passengers who had sea sickness.

"Lawd, me only have a few cents left. Norman, we nearly reach England. What are we going to do? You have any money?"

Norman fumbled through his pocket. He had six cents to be exact. The pair had spent all their money on drink. A little rum was what passed the time. The only thing to do was to drink. It also made them feel as if they were on the trip like everyone else, not as stowaways.

"Nuh worry yuhself, we'll sort something out when we get to England," Norman smiled reassuringly, patting Rudy on the back.

Those who know most about Jamaican immigration say that a West Indian communist or two make a rule of being on the station platform, ready with advice and free with addresses of accommodation. Indeed, it is suggested that the accommodation the Communists can offer to any young Jamaican who arrives more or less penniless and a little bewildered is rather more lavish than anything else to be had. The British Council takes good care to keep every student who has come here, out of harms way. On the whole, though, it seems that the Communists make no great headway with the immigrant artisans. It is not a political fortune that these immigrants have come here to make.
THE TIMES 4 OCTOBER 1954

Two days before they arrived at Southampton, Norman lost Rudy, he could not find him anywhere.

He ran up and down the decks searching for him, interrogating those who knew him.

"Morris, you seen Rudy?" He queried a man who they had been drinking with a couple of nights ago.

"No man, not since the other night."

"You sure?"

"Yes, man," the man muttered as he sauntered off.

A tall Grenadian man overheard the conversation. "Norman, you looking for Rudy? I see him, man. He get catch last night."

"You sure you have the right man?" puzzled Norman.

"Yes. Rudy. About so high. Dark complexion."

"So where they catch him?"

"Man, he fell asleep on deck."

"It was his own fault, me warn him," sighed Norman.

There was a buzz of excitement in the air. At the first word that land was nearing, most passengers had rushed to the upper deck trying to catch their first glimpse of England. Voices asked the same questions. "Do you think there will be people there to welcome us?"

"Me sister say some of the English are nice, but others are not so friendly?"

"Let me see if me can see Buckingham Palace, or the Tower of London. Me hear it's such a big building."

Norman could not share in their festivities. He had too much on his mind. How would he get ashore? What had happened to Rudy? Would he be sent back to Trinidad?

When passengers left the ship, they all had to file past
the captain showing their passports and a ticket
verifying that they were not stowaways. Norman of
course did not have a passport. He thought quickly.
While the captain and other officers were busy talking
to passengers, Norman carefully, but quickly, slipped
by.

"Good day Mr Phillips, I hope you have enjoyed
your trip and that Britain brings you all that you
seek," grinned the olive-skinned captain speaking with
an unfamiliar accent.

"Thank you, I hope so too," smiled Norman.

The passengers slowly trailed off the ship and
loaded into the boat train that would transport them
to St Pancras station in London. Young women in their
skimpy cotton dresses, which had been ideal for the
tropical climates, shivered as they waited to board the
train. Those who had been better informed came
prepared with overcoats and knitted pullovers.

"Rudy, boy!"

Norman spotted his friend at the end of the carriage
sitting comfortably between two young Grenadian
women. He pushed and squeezed through the packed
carriage towards him.

"You never think you can get rid of me that easily,"
Rudy beamed.

"How did you make it? "

"Well you know me can get outta any jam, man. But Norman, you know we have to pay for the train ride?"

"But we all outta money," frowned Norman.

Passengers could leave an address and send the money later, but they did not have an address to go to.

"Don't worry, let me go and talk to this man I was moving with while I was on the boat, he never knew I was a stowaway," smirked Norman.

He found the plump Antiguan man at the very end of the carriage. "Where you going?" Norman asked. "Gimme your address man, because when I get a job I'll come and check you, so you might get one in the same place."

The man scrawled his address on the back of an envelope and Norman rejoined Rudy. "Look what we're going to do, we'll say we lost our wallets, fumble like we looking for the ticket, then give him this address."

The inspector came around and they began to fumble. They handed over the address and promised to pay in three weeks. "Well, just forget that," they whispered in unison as the inspector wandered off.

One of the Paddington refreshment room windows early yesterday morning framed a picture of more than 300 West Indian immigrants pouring out of a Plymouth boat train, to be welcomed by about a same number of West Indian relatives and friends who have already established themselves in London. A group of porters sipped tea and watched the scene. 'It's wrong letting them come in,' said one of them. 'Thousands of us wanting houses and every week these West Indians

are coming in to make things worse.'"
THE TIMES 4 OCTOBER, 1954

The boat train slowly pulled into platform five. As the passengers poured out, the barriers were pushed aside and trunks, suitcases, boxes, baskets, hat boxes off-loaded and carelessly dumped to make way for animated reunions.

In the thick of the handshakes, kisses, laughter and confusion the lone travellers wandered struggling with their bags, half frightened by these strange surroundings and romantically yearned to spot a familiar face. Some were lucky enough to be steered in the direction of a help kiosk manned by a group of friendly-looking black gentlemen.

It had been the brainchild of Ivo De Souza an ex-serviceman from Jamaica who was now working for the Colonial Office. He was charged with the task of integrating the new arrivals into the British way of life and one of the ways was to recruit West Indians already living in England to meet them as they arrived. Some went to Liverpool and Portsmouth. Others were stationed at the main train stations in London.

When a train came into a London station, some would stroll confidently up to a cabby and demand to be taken to an address in Birmingham or Liverpool not knowing that travelling such distances in a black cab was nearly a week's wages. The drivers would send them to the help kiosk.

The men at the kiosk also explained to the new arrivals that, to find work, they would have to register at the Labour Exchange. They would find out what each applicant was capable of, then send them to an appropriate place of work.

Norman looked around. He felt strange. His treasured glorious yellow suit and wide brimmed hat and butter-coloured shoes seemed widely out of place amidst the muted greys and blues around him. A few of the perspiring railway porters, who had been ushered to transport baggage, eyed him curiously. Fortunately, through the crowd of expectant relatives and friends, Norman spotted a face from home, Frederick Ward, one of Trinidad's top boxers.

"Fred. Is that you, boy?"

"Norman. What? But wait? Me never knew you were coming to England. The last I hear you were in jail," said the muscular figure.

"Well it was a last minute thing, you know."

"You never see my sister on the boat, me come to meet her."

"You lie, me never see her."

"Where are you going? You have somewhere to stay?"

"No. You know of somewhere?"

"Come and stay with me. There's not much room, there are some other West Indians staying there, but it'll be fine."

"Great. Can Rudy come too?"

"No problem."

The flat was in a house owned by a Jewish man on Dunsmure Road, in Stamford Hill. Both the other men in the flat were working — one was a welder, the other in the Air Force. Between them they promised to give Norman and Rudy a couple of pounds every weekend when they got paid until they found a job.

LEN'S STORY

Your suggestion that Jamaicans might go to Nigeria as craftsmen is attractive. But, from my enquires, I am inclined to doubt whether it would really be practicable. One difficulty is that all informed opinion seems to agree that the Nigerian people themselves would not be likely to welcome an influx of immigrants.

I, however, agree most warmly with you that this is a serious problem and I can assure you that the Secretary of State for the Colonies is personally in close touch with all the Ministers concerned about the many difficult questions which arise from the influx of these British subjects.

PROPOSAL TO RESTRICT THE RIGHT OF BRITISH SUBJECTS FROM OVERSEAS TO ENTER AND REMAIN IN THE UNITED KINGDOM 20 DECEMBER 1954

Len Garrison was nine when his father left Jamaica for England. His mother left to join her husband a year later. They had told Len he would be sent for in a couple of years when they had made a good home, in the meantime he was enrolled at boarding school.

As a young carefree boy, Len had little perception of time. When his mother left, he thought she would be back within a couple of weeks. When the reality of her long term absence set in, Len felt scared and alone.

Growing up, there had always been plenty to eat — a pot of stewing curried meat on the stove, creamy home-made vanilla fudge in the cupboard, a jar full of his mother's delicious melt-in-the-mouth sugar cake in a jar. But at boarding school in Jamaica, pupils were confined to one predictable meal a day: a combination of rice, vegetables and some poor excuse for a piece of meat or fish.

At night when the rumbling in his stomach and the craving for something sweet got the better of him, Len would sneak out and prowl the streets of Kingston, hunting coconut ice cream, freshly roasted peanuts or a well-seasoned leg of chicken.

As a small boy, he was vulnerable on the streets alone. At night, Kingston came alive. Brazen women smeared with blood red lipstick strolled up and down beckoning to potential customers; burly middle aged men angrily stumbled out of rum shops. But Len never came to any harm. Though sometimes, slipping back through the open ground floor window, he got caught and was beaten.

At night Len lay awake in the dormitory that he shared with twelve other boys. He wanted his mother. He wrote her a letter pleading with her to come home. "Dear Mommie", he had scrawled. "I miss you so much. When are you coming home? School is such a horrible place . . . "

A couple of months later Len's aunt came to get him and he went to stay with family in the country. She was distressed at the gaunt, vulnerable figure that was now her nephew.

Most of the immigrant passengers who arrived in Paddington today from the Italian liner Auriga had relatives and friends waiting for them on the platform. It was plain to see that the newcomers had travelled in accordance with a family plan prepared by early comers . . .
THE TIMES 4 OCTOBER 1954

It was just after his twelfth birthday when Len finally boarded the vessel that would carry him to his mother and father. To a small boy, the ship seemed huge. It was loaded with mounds and mounds of green bananas that were strewn all over the deck, leaving barely enough room for the sixty or so passengers.

Len was in no doubt what a super place England would be. At school, teachers said that Jamaicans were originally African slaves who were brought to the Caribbean. "That can't be so," he thought. He much preferred to think of himself as a member of the British Commonwealth.

Africans were stupid, like the child in his Little Black Sambo book. The African boy was being chased by a tiger. He was chased round and round a tree and ended up being turned to butter. "Stupid boy", Len thought. His books about England romantically told of gallant, handsome princes rescuing beautiful princesses in distress. Len considered himself a prince, not a black Sambo.

From the offset there was a carnival atmosphere on the boat. A couple of the young men had brought guitars and they were singing and enticing the passengers to dance.

This activity provided the ideal opportunity for Len to give the old Methodist Minster, who had been appointed his travelling guardian, the slip. While the Minister reminisced about years long since gone, Len sloped off with a couple of boys his own age. There was too much fun to be had, they could not afford to waste any time.

The gang soon found a loose rope that made a good sturdy, but daring swing. Len patiently pushed the swing as the more dominant of the pack took their turn. Eventually it was his go. Len nervously hoisted himself into the contraption and waited to be pushed.

Backwards and forwards. Backwards and forwards. Len closed his eyes as the heavy hand swung him perilously near the edge of the ship.

Fortunately a man happened to be passing by and came to Len's rescue, putting an end to their risky game.

CONNIE'S STORY

The inflow of immigrants, mainly from the West Indies, has greatly increased. Colonial governments cannot be expected to control this flow and no limit to the numbers likely to come, particularly from Jamaica, is in sight. The only effective method of restricting these immigrants is to impose a form of control on entry and employment, including powers of deportation.

MEMORANDUM ON COLONIAL IMMIGRANTS FROM THE HOME SECRETARY TO THE CABINET **1954**

I circulate my memorandum suggesting that we should review what is being done to facilitate the further development of the resources in the West Indies so as to provide the maximum opportunity for West Indians, and so minimise one of the causes of the influx to this country.

COLONIAL OFFICE MEMORANDUM **8 FEBRUARY 1955**

When Connie Goodridge arrived at London Airport from Jamaica one chilly November morning in 1954, there was only one thing on her mind. She had not seen her husband Stanley for seven months. He was a fast bowler and had been to England to play for a team in Durham called St Harbour.

She had missed him so much. Especially when she had given birth to their daughter Amru. It had been a difficult labour. Connie had been at the University College Hospital for almost seventy-two hours. She was a medical secretary at the institution, so the staff had made sure she received the best attention.

The labour pains kept coming and going, coming and going. Through a drug-induced daze Connie heard the doctors whispering. One of them then said to her clearly that they were going to have to perform a caesarean section.

There were of course letters. Every day Stanley's father would come and look for Connie to see if his son had written. Connie would read him the letters. His eyes would light up when he heard how well his son was doing in England.

But letters could no way make up for him not being there, and Amru was now three months old, it was time she saw her father. So Connie packed her bags and flew to England to persuade her man to come home where he belonged.

Connie MacDonald had met Stanley Goodridge when she was twenty-two at a dance in the village of Bournemouth.

"Larry, who's that guy over there, the tall one in the light suit," Connie had whispered to her friend.

"It's Stanley Goodridge, the cricketer. You know he

has played for Jamaica a few times. Why? You like him. I could always introduce you to him."

A few minutes later, Stanley was walking over towards Connie.

"Good evening, I'm Stanley Goodridge," he outstretched his hand towards Connie.

"Hello, I'm Connie MacDonald." She smiled, he was so tall and handsome.

That was how it all began with Stanley, but he was not Connie's first love. He was her second. Carl had been her first. Since most could remember it had been a forgone conclusion that Connie and Carl would get married. They suited each other so well. They looked good together. Came from the same background. Shared similar hobbies.

But then Connie went away for a week. When she came back her friends told her that a woman from the next town had vowed that if she saw the right man for her daughters, she would work all sorts of magic to get them together. And she thought Carl was ideal for one of her daughters. Connie laughed. A few months later, Carl married one of the woman's daughters.

Connie had been so humiliated. When she went to town, people quizzed her.

"But wait. Connie, I thought you and Carl were going to be married?"

"Yes, Mrs Martin, but it did not work out."

So Connie married Stanley. He was five years her junior, a fact which her newly acquired mother-in-law never failed to bring up.

As a cricketer, Stanley was so well-known and Connie was proud. To her, he was one of the best cricketers Jamaica had. When he was overlooked for the West Indies side during a tour of England in favour of Alfred Valentine, Connie told everyone that he should have been picked instead of this Trinidadian who did nothing on the tour except play the piano.

But with all his fame, Stanley was shy. People always wanted his autograph which he hated. But Connie was always ready to soak up the limelight.

As soon as Connie came out of Customs, she spotted Stanley standing in the middle of a crowd waiting for friends and family. He was so tall and handsome, carrying a fabulous white fur jacket for baby Amru.

Connie fiddled with her hair and smoothed down the dress that she had meticulously chosen to make her husband realise how much he was missing.

The couple looked at each other lovingly. Then with their daughter lodged firmly between them, passionately kissed. Connie held on to Stanley tightly. This time she was not going to let go.

Connie was blissfully ignorant that the joy of being reunited with the man of her dreams would quickly wear off, when the reality of life in England sunk in.

To the Editor of THE TIMES,
Sir, Parliament's decision to set up a Committee of Guidance to deal with the problems arising from the large influx of West Indians into this country seems

unfortunately characteristic of the Government's myopic colonial policy. Poverty and unemployment in Jamaica, appear to have been overlooked.

Proposals to help immigrants when once in England are all very well, but surely an increase in capital investment and in orders for West Indian sugar, to keep the industry at its peak and all the consequent prosperity would drastically reduce the number of immigrants and help free the West Indies from further Communist encroachments.

YOURS FAITHFULLY ROLAND DALLAS, FORT GEORGE, KENT.

Old slabs of wood blocked the stairway to Number Fifty-three. A black man perched on the downstairs window sill smoking a cigarette. He nodded his head to acknowledge Stanley Goodridge who ushered his wife and daughter through the battered door.

Inside, the paint work oozed with black speckles of mould and a damp rotten stench suffocated the air. Carrying Amru, Stanley steered his wife up the wooden staircase, holding her by the waist so she did not lose her footing on the broken steps.

"Stanley, you mean we must live here?" Connie cried, eyeing the tiny box room.

"Trust me, Connie. It was the best me could find for me money. Don't worry, we'll look for something else."

That night, no matter how many layers she wrapped up in, the cold still found its way into her bones.

For the first few weeks the Goodridges stayed in this box room in a house for single men. Gentlemen co-habiting with women was against the rules, but the landlord had kindly given Connie and Stanley two weeks to find somewhere more suitable. Back in Jamaica, Connie had drifted off to sleep to the soft chirping of crickets and rustle of palm trees. In Britain, the constant sounds of the busy city streets kept her wide awake. There was also the echoes of the house to contend with. Most of the men who lived there worked and slept on a shift basis. When one was at work, another slept in his bed. When he returned, he went to bed and the other went to work. The constant movement stirred Connie from her sleep, not to mention the stale food smells. Connie could not get used to sleeping in the same room she ate in. To make it easier, on a mild evening, they would buy fish and chips wrapped in newspapers and eat them on a park bench. But on an average night, the aroma of stewing mutton mixed with oil from the paraffin heater would linger on.

"Stanley, you mean to say me left my big house inna Jamaica with a back yard, maid and gardener for this?" Connie had argued. Their circumstances forced her to question why she had come to England. But looking into Stanley's soft brown eyes, she knew the answer.

Within a few weeks of keeping her ear to the ground,

Connie heard talk of a room going in Chelsea, that had a bath. A bath was important to Connie. England was so dirty she had to keep her baby clean. But it seemed that hygiene was not a priority for the British. Some days before, she had turned down a room in Cunningham Road because it didn't have a bath.

"You should take what you can get," the landlady had warned her.

Mrs Smith was the lady of the house in Chelsea. At first, the middle aged woman seemed reluctant to take on black lodgers. After a barrage of intrusive questions, her desire for two pounds five shillings a week proved stronger than her distrust of immigrants.

As soon as she fished in her flowery pinafore and wrote out a receipt for the five pounds deposit, Mrs Smith laid down the rules of the house. One bath a week, on a Thursday. "And God help you if you drip one bit of water," she warned peering over the top of her round spectacles.

Under no circumstances could the room be altered. The room had a bed and a wash basin in it, that was it. If they brought a chair into the room, she would charge them for it. They had use of the kitchen, which did not have a fridge. If Connie wanted to keep anything chilled, she would have to put it out on the window sill. Finally, Connie had to scrub the staircase on Fridays.

The bath was in the dining area, and when it was not

in use, a piece of wood was covered over it and Mrs Smith and her husband used it as a chair.

But it was not so bad. The public baths were just around the corner, on North End Road. Connie and her family would go and bathe there on a Saturday morning. There was a little room at the back which was seldom used. Inside, Connie would fill the bucket up with three kettles full of hot water and then they would take it in turns to lather each other's skin and have a good scrub in all the necessary parts that needed to be scrubbed. Then they washed off the soap suds. It was her and Stanley's little game.

"Mrs Goodridge, Mrs Goodridge," Mrs Smith was calling. Connie was in the kitchen singing along to Ella Fitzgerald on the wireless. She had decided on soup for dinner. She was chopping up some meat to go with the red peas that Mrs Charles had sent her from Jamaica. Unlike many of the West Indians she had met in England, the English food agreed with her. As long as she had rice, that was fine. But if there was one thing Connie did miss from home it was red peas. Once she got hold of some, she prized them like gold and saved them for special occasions then stewed the peas with cuts of meat or cooked up a large pot of rice and peas.

"Mrs Goodridge are you cooking?" Mrs Smith popped her scarf covered head around the door.

"Yes, Mrs Smith. Is there a problem with that?"

"No dear, but I can hear the wireless on in your room. You know both the cooker and radio uses so much electricity. Can I suggest that you turn the wireless off while you are in the kitchen. You can turn it back on when you go back to your room."

"Okay, Mrs Smith." Connie went to switch the radio off.

"Oh, and Mrs Goodridge, don't forget to wash the stairs in the landing tomorrow morning. There's a love."

"No, I won't Mrs Smith. And Mrs Smith . . . " Connie mumbled under her breath, mimicking the old woman's cockney accent, " . . . you're so god damn ignorant."

"Pardon, luvvie?"

"Nothing, Mrs Smith."

The Goodridge family soon moved from the house in Chelsea. That's the way it usually was. They would stay somewhere for a short period of time then hear about somewhere better, and move.

Connie had this joke with a friend in Scotland. They had two pages for each other in their respective address books, because they moved around so much. It was easy. They did not have any furniture to move, only clothes and a few kitchen utensils. Still, there was fun to be had out of the situation.

Connie made friends with a white woman called Susan who became her assistant in her flat-hunting endeavours. Connie would ask to see a room and the landlady would invariably tell her that it had already gone. Then Susan would ask to see the room, to which she would get the response, "Come in, dear. Here let me show you around."

Then Connie would go back to the same landlady and demand to know why she was treated differently. "It's your house, you can do what you like, but why do you have to lie?"

Some of the white residents resent having coloured people move in as fellow tenants. To their protest they have added secondhand stories, of 10 Jamaicans sleeping in one room, of knife fights, immoral practices and drug trafficking.

No-one I talked to had first-hand evidence of these stories. None were willing to be quoted. Probably because they were wrong.

The truth is that Brixton's Little Harlem is settling down very nicely. Police say there is less trouble in the area than there was three years ago.

Their regard for the West Indian woman is particularly high — 'steady, home-loving respectable women. Look at the way they dress and look after their children. And you never see them in the pubs.'
EVENING STANDARD 6 OCTOBER 1954

"Connie, my contract has been renewed for another year. It looks like we staying in England a while longer," Stanley Goodridge matter-of-factly said as he tucked into his porridge one morning. Connie looked up from spooning stewed apples into Amru's reluctant mouth.

"You're joking. I don't think I can stay another day

in England. This place is so depressing and dreary. Please, let's go back home. You can still play cricket and I can go back to work at the hospital."

"No, my mind's made up. And I already told them I would be staying, Connie. It'll be okay."

Connie Goodridge had been in England for four months. She had cried for most of that time. She missed her family and the life she was accustomed to. In her eyes, she had come down in life.

"Connie, maybe if you get a job things will not seem so bad." Stanley got up and walked toward the kitchen, signalling that the conversation was over.

Many of the employers who co-operated with the Ministry of Labour in finding jobs for the EMPIRE WINDRUSH men, for example, have informed the Ministry of Labour that newly arrived coloured workers tend to be quarrelsome among themselves and to react violently to real or imaginary affronts. The trouble that this is causing amongst existing workers is one of the number of reasons why many employers are reluctant to use coloured labour to relieve even the most persistent labour shortages.

We therefore recommend that no organised large scale immigration of male Colonial workers should be contemplated; arrangements must be made for the immigration of a limited number of female Colonial workers for employment as hospital domestics.
PRO LAB 26/226

Connie was determined to get a job as a medical secretary, after all that was what she was trained for. But her first experiences were not promising.

"Good morning, my name is Connie Goodridge," she said in her poshest voice. "I'm calling to find out if you have any vacancy at the hospital. I have worked as . . . "

"Are you coloured?" asked the anonymous voice at the end of the telephone line.

"Yes. Is that a problem?"

"You coloured people come here and think the streets are paved with gold," the woman quickly replied.

"Well if the streets in England are paved with gold, how come you are working at a hospital?" Connie slammed down the receiver and stormed out of the phone box.

Connie had called up so many agencies looking for work. Invariably they would speak to her very slowly, dragging out every syllable. "One, I'm not deaf and, two, I do speak English," Connie would reply. At one agency, Connie was told to stay on the line while the agent found out if the job was still going. Connie could hear her asking the employer on the other line, if they minded being sent a black person for the job.

"They don't mind taking you on, but they don't know your level of education," the agency worker informed Connie when she came back on the line.

This made Connie's blood boil. The examinations back home were the same as in England. In fact, all the exam papers were sent to England to be marked.

It was these little things that really began to irritate

her. People assumed that because she was not the same colour, she was ignorant and did not speak the same language. She then applied for a job at St Mary's Hospital in Paddington. "It's not our policy to employ coloured secretaries," she was told. If she had been a nurse that would have been all right and if she was a maid that was all right. But no way would they have a black secretary.

Connie was determined to find a job. She had an interview at the National Hospital for Nervous Diseases in Queen's Square. One of the women on her interview panel quizzed, 'Do you have a good command of the English language?' Connie put her shoulders back and proudly said, 'Well I should hope so, madam, because it's the only language I know.'

After Connie had started the job, one of her colleagues informed her that she had been appointed largely because of the bold way she had answered.

DORIS'S STORY

Little Harlem lies 300 yards from Brixton's bustling market. Its Labour Exchange is the first port of call for West Indian immigrants.

Here brown-skinned men stand in groups talking with a soft drawl. Women walk by with the luxuriant easy stroll of the Caribbean.

Last month 177 new arrivals registered with the Labour Exchange at Brixton, bringing the total to nearly 1,000. The manager of the Brixton Labour Exchange said that every one of a September shipload of 80 West Indians had found a job within three weeks. 'Most of them are good workers,' he said. 'Employers are glad to have them.'
EVENING STANDARD **6 OCTOBER 1954**

Doris Rankin ran her hands through her hair. The harsh wind, the hard water and poor diet were taking its toll on her appearance. No matter how much she hot combed her hair to make it straight, it kinked and did not look right.

Doris had tried to find someone to set her hair in rollers for her. She walked pass hairdressing salons

filled with pampered white women drinking cups of
tea. Doris was almost tempted to go in, until a couple
of the stylists saw her looking through the window.
Their harsh glances made it clear she was not
welcome.

"You all right?" A black woman sat down in the
aisle opposite Doris on the upper deck of the Luton-
bound bus. The women smiled at each other.

"Fine."

"I haven't seen you around here before. My name's
Doris Rankin."

The woman shook Doris' outstretched hand.

"Penelope Williams. I just come from Jamaica."

"Which village ya from?"

"Manderville. Me just come over a few months ago
to join me husband."

"I'm from Portland. I came to England after the
Coronation in 1953."

Doris' stop was fast approaching. She could not
afford to miss it. It was a long walk back.

"Darling, give me your address. Do you have
paper?"

"No. Quick. Write it on me hand. I'll transfer it
later."

"Penelope Williams, 12 Bury Avenue, Luton," the
woman scrawled with a fountain pen.

"My stop. You'll hear from me soon, Penelope."

"Bye".

That was the way it was up in Bedfordshire. Doris
hardly saw any other black people. When she did it

was usually on the bus. They always rushed to exchange addresses before their destination. She and her husband had found a small room to rent in a semi-detached house in the centre of Bedford. The rent was reasonable, as was the condition of the room. But Mrs Tyler, the landlady, was tiresome. She treated them like children and refused to give them a key to the front door. "What time you coming back, Mrs Rankin?" she would ask.

Mrs Tyler would wait up for them to come in, and if that was after six in the evening, they would be locked out and would have to find somewhere else to stay the night. After dark they were shut up in the small 10 foot by 12 foot room with a temperamental wireless. Not that there was that much to do. Everything closed at five in the evening. The public houses had limited opening hours, and there was no gambling. Sometimes on a Sunday she went with her 10-year-old daughter and husband on a long sixpence bus ride, or for a stroll just to get the exercise.

Doris missed her family, friends, the barbecues on the beaches, swimming in the ocean. She had given up so much. Back home she had been a business woman owning a restaurant and a grocers. She also owned a house with a large yard, yet had given it all up for the sake of her husband, who had wanted to come to England. She knew she had to survive. A friend who lived in London had told of how some Jamaicans had become so homesick that they had fallen ill and were hospitalised. Doris was determined that a similar fate would not befall her.

"Do you have any cassava or green banana, please."

"You what? No, none of that foreign stuff here, love. We only have what you see. Good old English fruit and veg."

Doris' eyes roamed over the selection of produce. Potatoes, cabbage, brussels sprouts, cauliflower. They all tasted the same, as far as she was concerned. Doris picked up a cabbage. As she held it up, the brown, wilted leaves drooped down.

"Don't you have anything fresher?" she asked.

"You people should be bloody grateful to come here and be able to eat the produce of a civilised country," came the reply. "Some of your people are still eating each other, aren't they? How about some nice brussels sprouts, love?"

Doris inspected the vegetable, maybe she could do a little something with them.

Back home, the pumpkin she had planted before she emigrated would be ready for picking just about now, she mused.

"Okay, I'll take some brussels sprouts," she decided finally.

Most of the other women bought their goods on credit from the grocers, and paid a little each week. But Doris was reluctant to do this. In Jamaica she had always frowned on the 'buy now, pay later' method of making ends meet, even though it would have made her money stretch a little further. Her husband earned about four pounds a week, Doris three pounds. The rent was three pounds. And after paying a child minder one pound and ten shillings to look after her daughter, there was not much left.

In Jamaica, rearing children would not have been a problem. You had people around. You could go about your work and neighbours would mind the children.

WHERE'S YOUR TAIL?

As for the British West Indies, the fact is that would-be immigrants are all in practice Negroes. It seems to us very understandable that America should want to limit the flow of Negro immigrants where practicable.

Nor does it make much sense to argue that West Indians should continue to be admitted under the United Kingdom quotas, since their race raises a problem which immigration from the British Isles does not.

EXTRACT FROM A CONFIDENTIAL LETTER FROM THE BRITISH EMBASSY IN WASHINGTON TO THE FOREIGN OFFICE
17 AUGUST 1955

Len Garrison was trying to fit in at school. Today was his first swimming lesson. Although he came from an island surrounded by water, Len had never learnt to swim. Fitted in the new navy-coloured trunks his mother had just bought from Woolworth's, Len stood, shivering at the pool side, waiting for the teacher's instructions. His new life was taking some adjusting to. Since he arrived in England, it was like they were all living in a kind of secrecy. The strangers in the streets were in too much of a hurry to stop and say hello. They all scurried into their houses then shut their doors firmly behind them. Everything was locked up and hidden away. Len wondered what went on behind the closed doors. Back home everyone always had time for each other. Neighbours left their doors ajar as an open invitation for friends to drop in. In England, however, he other children who lived in his street were white. They looked at him and whispered loud enough for Len to hear:

"Golliwog, Sambo, Monkey, Blackie . . . Where's your tail . . . ? Does the black wash off . . . ?" At home he had been ignorant of the significance of colour.

But the cruel chants of the children were nothing compared to what he was to experience at school. Len had been enrolled at the respectable all-boy institution, Paul Kingsley School in Chelsea. It was a cold, tall, concrete building with endless corridors. Len doubted he would ever be able to find his way around. It was so different from the village school back home where he had known everybody. At Paul Kingsley School, he was the only black boy.

From the very first day Len was constantly victimised — tripped up, called names and so on. In the playground some of the other pupils would recite passages from the popular story book by Enid Blyton, *Three Golliwogs:* "There were once three golliwogs — Nigger, Golly and Woggie, who were most unhappy in the nursery cupboard. None of the other toys liked them because their mistress, Angela, did not like black faces . . . "

The first couple of times, he had complained to his form teacher, Mr Gray, who brushed it off and put the bullying down to Len's reluctance to 'fit in'. So the name calling, the pranks and the tripping up went on and on. Then one school morning someone thrust Len a pair of boxing gloves and the next moment he was forced in a ring to 'fight it out' in two three minute rounds. He came off worse.

He went home bruised physically and emotionally. "There's no point explaining to mother and father, they don't understand," he thought.

Len tried to fit in. He joined the school choir and enjoyed it. The choir was due to perform at a concert. They had been rehearsing for weeks. Days before the event, someone had started a fight in the playground. The teacher decided that Len would not be allowed to attend the concert, as he was to blame for the playground incident. Although another teacher took up the matter with the head master, saying that Len was being used as a scapegoat, Len nevertheless missed the concert. One or two boys later stretched out the hand of friendship, but Len was still convinced the whole school was against him.

Len continued to wait patiently for his first swimming lesson to begin. Then suddenly a group of boys surrounded him and shoved him in the deep end of the pool. Len desperately tried to stop himself from falling in, but it was too late. As he hit the water, all he could hear was the echo of their laughter. To him it seemed like a lifetime, but in reality it was only a few seconds before a boy jumped in and pulled him out. As Len was hauled out of the water, he was greeted by a sea of laughing white faces. Mr Gray was laughing too, he did not even ask how the pupil was. Len wanted to cry, but fought the tears back. "This is a dangerous environment. Life in England is all about survival," told himself.

"COLOUR BAR GETTING THINNER"

FROM OUR CORRESPONDENT

BIRMINGHAM, OCT. 13

More than 100 Jamaicans arrived in Birmingham throughout the day, but by late this afternoon most of them had vanished into the city and outlying areas. Birmingham's liaison officer to the coloured population in the city, Mr. W. J. Davis, was left to find accommodation for only 13.

To the question of whether the Jamaicans will readily find work, an official of the regional employment exchange said that there would be no difficulty in placing the men and women at this stage. Indeed, some employers had been so satisfied with coloured workers that they had asked for more. There was opportunity for both skilled and unskilled.

"I think the colour bar is getting thinner and thinner in the Midlands. There are so many coloured people in Birmingham now that their arrival is no longer a novelty," the official added.

WHITE WOMEN/BLACK MEN

More than two-thirds of Britain's white population held a low opinion of black people or disapproved of them. They saw them as heathens who practiced head-hunting, cannibalism, infanticide, polygamy and black magic.

They saw them as uncivilised, backward people inherently inferior to Europeans, living in primitive huts 'in the bush', wearing few clothes, eating strange food and suffering from unpleasant diseases. They saw them as ignorant and illiterate, speaking strange languages, and lacking proper education.

They believed that black men had stronger sexual urges than white men, were less inhibited, and could give greater satisfaction to their partners.

PETER FRYER, STAYING POWER **1984**

Norman Phillips was adjusting well to the English nightlife, though it had taken some getting used to at first. At parties, there was only white women and black guys and white guys. Black women were not

seen in such places. It was considered inappropriate.
The black women he tried to greet on the street did not
acknowledge him. He felt as though they were snobby,
with their heads up in the clouds. However bad the
situation, friends told him that it was even worse a few
years ago when there were hardly any West Indian
women in England. Most of those who came over now
were looking to better themselves, and that did not
include mixing with the single black men who were
just out for a good time. "Don't worry," one friend
maintained, there was still fun to be had with the
white women who welcomed these black men with
their sharp dress sense and fancy footwork. Though
seeing white women jiving together in the clubs did
perplex Norman, it just did not happen in Trinidad.

Things in the women's department were working out
quite nicely. Norman and Rudy had moved out of the
crowded flat in Dunsmure Road into a room of their
own. It was so crowded, in fact, that whenever
Norman wanted to take a girl home, Rudy stayed out
on the streets. And if Rudy had a lady friend in the
room, Norman would quickly make himself scarce.

Most of Norman's night prowling took place in the
East End. He was a regular at the St Louis club on
Cable Street. Each visit the African owner, Sheriff,
would have to lay down the law with Norman and his
friends about drinking after hours. Norman could not
understand, why there was a curfew on his drinking.

But between the legitimate hours Norman's motto was: "We drink till we pass out."

Norman had arrived in the autumn when the weather was fairly mild, a woollen jumper sufficiently kept out the night chill. But now with the early morning frost, winter was setting in and Norman needed a coat. He wanted a fur one like the type he saw the office men wearing on their way to their jobs in the city. Then on the way from a long shift at Gamidges delivery service in Holborn, Norman spotted the fur coat he had been looking for. It was beige, double-breasted with a big collar and deep pockets for his cold hands. The price tag read nine pounds. It was a lot of money, but Norman had been saving for a few weeks.

"Perfect. It hangs just right on you. You will be the envy of your friends," the shopkeeper said, flattering his potential customer.

"Yes, yes, I think you're right," Norman swaggered, as he eyed himself admiringly in the mirror.

"Take off that coat. That is a woman's thing," shouted Sam, as Norman walked boldly through the pub doors in his new coat. Like on most evenings the Caribbean boys were propping up the bar, nursing a round of shorts after a hard day's work.

"Me never know you like wearing woman clothes, Norman. Or is it Norma? Your secret is safe with us," Michael jested, as he doubled over laughing. "Don't come near me, me not into that thing."

His vanity turned to embarrassment, as Norman's friends continued to laugh and cuss over his new purchase.

"I've worn it all the way from the store. Me never know it was a woman coat," Norman helplessly protested.

The shopkeeper had duped Norman into purchasing a woman's coat.

"People will think me is a homosexual. I must get rid of it," he decided.

Taking it back to the shop would have been too humiliating. Norman stormed out of the pub and tossed the fur coat on the nearest heap of rubbish.

Later, spruced up for a night on the town Norman, Sam, Michael and Winston made their way to Cato's, a club in the East End owned by a Maltese guy.

The others noisily amused themselves in a heavy drinking session and scanned the club for any available women. But Norman was distracted. The fur coat was still bugging him and the cold made it even worse. He began dancing, but the coat continued to plague his mind.

"Don't let this go on," the headline read. "This place is a veritable den of iniquity."

Robert Murray chuckled to himself as he read the article in the daily newspaper slating the Paramount dance hall.

The article said the men who frequented the place

were peddlers of dope and dealers in guns, and even hinted that the women were nothing less than tarts. It suggested the club should be bombed.

Robert had been going to the Paramount since his early days in the Royal Air Force. The club on Tottenham Court Road in the West End, close to Warren Street Underground station, was owned by the Mecca entertainment organisation and had always been popular with military men when they got leave or 48-hour passes.

It was situated in the very depths of a large basement, with plush decor consisting of sparkling chandeliers, gold panelled walls, and there was always live music, sometimes two big bands. The Paramount was one of the few places where black men could go without getting hassled. It was also where many of them met the women who were later to become their wives.

But the newspaper had a field day, talking about "ill-timed and unwanted fraternising", but the real problem was that the reporter did not like black men mixing with white women.

Women who befriended the West Indians were a much maligned body of people, often objects of derision, jibes and taunts. Yet, they never wavered in their allegiance and loyalty when the going got tough and, as far as Robert was concerned, no amount of praise was too high for them. They were a tower of strength and among the few British people who had extended the hand of welcome to West Indians.

"Many loves have been lost and made in the Paramount," Robert mused after reading the newspaper article. After all, he had met Johanna in the Paramount and, who knows, she might just end up being the woman he would spend the rest of his life with . . .

Cecil Holness had also found love at the Paramount. Clara had been born in England. Coincidentally her father was from the same town in Jamaica where Cecil's family lived. He had fought in the First World War and later settled in Britain. Clara's mother was English. The couple planned to get married two years later.

Aside from the romantic pull of the Paramount, it was also where Jimmy Munro's cricket team met every afternoon to discuss new tactics so they could once and for all defeat the might of Learie Constantine's West Indian eleven.

"If you open the innings, Andre, play some nice defensive shots. Don't be too adventurous. We want to last the duration."

"Well, I think I should be given a chance to open the innings," interrupted Charlie.

"No, man, let's go with Andre and Douglas. They play well and can pave the way for Raggy and Flash."

Charlie sat back in his chair as Johnny finished writing out the team picked for Saturday's friendly against sugar manufacturer Tate and Lyle's eleven in his black book. He was the captain and had the final say.

A few years back, Jimmy Munro had won nearly eighty thousand pounds in the football pools. He had bought two very large buildings in Earl's Court, west London, to house West Indian ex-servicemen and new arrivals from the Caribbean. Each property had five floors and a basement.

But a West Indian's first love is his cricket, so it naturally followed that Jimmy set up his own team.

Johnny Griffiths was the skipper and Raggy Phillips, Dinky Munro, Robert "Flash" Murray, Andre Shervington and Arthur Dujon made up the core of the team which registered in the national club cricket conference as medium to strong.

Most of the team, like Andre, had honed their cricketing skills in England during their stint in the Royal Air Force.

The RAF had wanted to keep the men occupied after the hostilities had ended so organised competitions between the different bases.

Back in 1945, Andre had been at RAF Rey, in Kent. They had organised a match between the crew and their superiors. Andre had batted well at number three, and with Flash Murray and Arthur Dujon to follow, they could not lose the game. With a victory under their belt, they eagerly took on challenges from other bases. The only problem was that the cool climate of England was so different from back home. Andre found it difficult to catch cricket balls with cold hands. But he adapted. Cricket was in his blood.

Back home in British Guiana, Andre lived in a large two storey, five bedroom house with his mother and father and six brothers and sisters.

The house was surrounded by a large yard, which their father decided should be a place for the children to play. It was the only house in the square of tenements where there was no other property in the back yard and children could play freely, so they all came. Over the years, so many children played on the ground that grass struggled to grow and the dusty earth crumbled under their feet.

Cricket was always the game played in the yard. As the youngest, Andre spent most of his time trying to fight his way into the team. Two tip a run was the favourite game. Batsmen were allowed to hit the ball twice and if they did not make a run, they were out.

The fence that encased the land made a good boundary line. If they ball was struck over the fence, the batsmen were out. Batsmen also had to hit the ball away from the fruit trees, especially the treasured banana tree, otherwise Mr Shervington would march out with his cane stick, and licks would be handed out all round.

Back in London, Andre was slumped drunkenly next to the statue of Eros. The animated neon displays of Piccadilly flashed on and off in a continual blur. He shook his head trying to re-focus and briefly caught a glimpse of a bunch of late night theatre goers.

Andre tried hard to concentrate so he could

remember the way to the bus that would carry him home. But all he could recall was the contagious melody of a calypso from back home about a prostitute.

Jimmy Munro's eleven usually played beer matches where the team with the least runs had to buy beer for the winning side. This match was different. Even through there was rationing, bottles and bottles of rum and good food had been laid on by Tate and Lyle, free of charge. And the men had taken full advantage of this hospitality.

"Excuse me, sir, are you all right? Can I be of any assistance?"

Andre looked up to see a policeman stooping over him.

"I . . . I . . . bus," Andre blurted out.

"I don't think you are in any state to catch the bus. I'm feeling generous, if you can tell me where you live, I'll drop you home."

The policeman put his arms around Andre and helped him up and into a Black Maria police van.

BURN NIGGER BURN

Kensington has a colour problem whether you care to admit it or not. It must exist where people of greatly differing outlook, emotions and appearance are living side by side. Petty problems become magnified out of all proportions so the fact that a Jamaican cooks a strong-smelling stew and a lucky lad from Trinidad wins the pools and buys a luxury car, becomes a festering sore of complaint and jealousy.
KENSINGTON NEWS AND WEST LONDON TIMES
AUGUST 29 1958

Andre Shervington turned left into Clarendon Road heading north towards Blenheim Crescent, carefully dodging the broken glass and bricks that littered the streets. He paused and looked behind him. It was only a ten minute journey, but he could not be too careful.

Night was beginning to fall and curtains at the windows of black homes in Notting Hill twitched with African and Caribbean families nervously wondering what the evening would bring.

They had good reason to approach the enveloping

THE NEWS' FORECAST
RACE TROUBLES —Says Trades Council

'Home Office Should Have Taken Notice'

Colville Road Flare-up

AT a meeting of Kensington and Hammersmith Trades Council on Wednesday, Mr. C. T. McCarthy (T.G.W.U.), said that the 'Kensington News' through the intuition of its reporters, had foreseen the Notting Hill race riots several weeks before they actually happened. The Home Office, he said, should have taken notice of what the "Kensington News" had had to say about the conditions and brewing storm in North Kensington.

He said that colour riots were getting this country a bad name in international circles, and regretted that the Notting Hill Gate episodes should have hit the headlines. He went on : "I offer my personal sympathies to no coloured people in this era of fear. The coloured man, unlike the Irishman or the Welshman, is so conspicuous. I have seen things in North Kensington recently that I never want to see again."

He concluded by saying : "The forces of law and order have been challenged . . . by teenagers who have no sense of responsibility." Once again, the speaker expressed his personal sympathy for the coloured people in all they had been through, and all they had suffered recently. "I think they behaved magnificently," he added.

"Certain elements, coloured and white, are trying to turn North Kensington into a Red Light area," said Mr. R. C. Greenwood (N.U.V.B.). "We don't believe we can get anywhere by riots." He went on to advocate action on the part of the authorities, and legislation to "Stop people doing wrong in this area."

Replying to this statement, Mr. R. W. Davies (C.S.C.A.) said that anyone who thinks that prostitution came to Notting Hill with the coloured people is just misinformed. Mr. Davies said that Notting Hill had always been the "battleground of North London," and "an area of vice and disturbance." As regards

Twenty teenage boys chased four coloured men in Colville Road on Sunday night.—Milk bottles were thrown as the four dived for safety into a nearby house, and broken glass was scattered over the pavement. Once inside the coloured men replied with more milk bottles thrown from the windows. Glass splinters flying hit a white man who was walking with his wife and baby in a pram, cutting his hands. When the police arrived the white youths had fled but statements were taken from the coloured men.

Assault On P.C. —Charge

A 26-year-old coloured student, Atkin Thomas, of Romilly Road, Finsbury Park, was accused at West London on Monday of assaulting P.C. Keith Golding whilst in the execution of his duty at Ladbroke Grove, North Kensington, in the early hours of Sunday morning. He was also charged with using insulting words whereby a breach of the peace may have been occasioned.

The student pleaded not guilty to the charges and was remanded in his own bail of £50 until September darkness with a sense of apprehension. There was talk every morning of yet another white gang armed with broken milk bottles, iron bars and knives beating black folk, smashing the windows of their houses and pouring petrol through their letterboxes during the night.

It was not safe to walk the streets after dark without an escort. Even then there was no guarantee of protection. These gangs were out "nigger hunting" and roamed in packs of twenty, fifty, a hundred even. They always out-numbered their prey.

Andre had grown accustomed to the whispered remarks in the street as he strolled passed groups of white faces congregated on the corner. But he could not comprehend how these passing insults had escalated into full-scale warfare with menacing letters stuffed into the mail boxes warning Grenadian families to "clear off or face the consequences"; Jamaicans being battered with clubs of wood; Trinidadians being slashed in the face with kitchen knives; and the crude home-made petrol bombs thrown through the windows of Antiguan family homes, while babies slept, oblivious to the ensuing danger.

Only the night before Johnson Joseph, a 23-year-old Dominican, had been set upon by a gang of white youths. He came out of Ladbroke Grove Station, turned right into Lancaster Road and became aware of footsteps behind him. As his pace quickened, so did that of his pursuers. By the time he got to the end of Lancaster Road, he was cornered.

To the joyous cries of "lynch the bleedin' nigger" the

youths relentlessly smashed him over the head with iron bars. The Dominican put his hands up to defend himself, but his brave efforts were futile.

A few moments later he was lying face down, choking in a pool of watery vomit and crimson blood. Though barely conscious, he could just make out the celebratory bragging and boasting of his attackers over whose blows had inflicted the most damage.

Night and day, Black Marias filled with weary policemen cruised the streets. But what good was this wondered Andre. There was talk that the police themselves were coming under attack and, in any case, he doubted whether they were on the West Indians' side.

Black people were being attacked, they reported the incidents, the police did nothing. Consequently the numbers of attacks began to escalate. Black families were virtually prisoners in their homes.

Mr Samuel Augustus Thomas, a coloured café owner described at Clerkenwell Magistrates Court how a gang of boys smashed up his café in Askew Road, Shepherd's Bush.

'Some came on foot, some in a car. They were armed with sticks. They rushed in and while I stood at the foot of the stairs, they used sticks, tables and chairs to smash up the place.'

Three boys were identified by Thomas and picked up in the street. 'You are not going to take the word of

Race Riot

Two policemen, one a handler with his dog, obviously at the ready, stop a youth in Lancaster Road, North Kensington, on Monday night at the height of the disturbances. He was suspected of being a member of a gang that attacked a coloured man.

a black man against three whites?' They asked.
KENSINGTON NEWS AND WEST LONDON TIMES
AUGUST 8 1958

Some saw the "nigger-bashers" as simply teenage teddy boys living up to their rock and roll lifestyle of gratuitous violence, rebellion and anti-establishment. For Andre and most of the other West Indians it was clear the blame rested with one individual, Oswald Mosley. His fascist Union Movement regularly met at Kensington Church Street.

While shopping in Portobello Market, Andre had stumbled across a lone white man armed with leaflets, preaching a message of black people spreading vice and disease in England, not to mention taking "our jobs and women". His leaflets depicted a cartoon of a black man wearing a grass skirt and carrying a spear.

Andre sensed Mosley's message was taking root. In the lower white working class stronghold of Notting Dale that bordered North Kensington. The day Mosley made a political speech in the local town hall, according to newspaper reports, some six hundred people had turned up to hear his racist theories.

Extra patrols were on duty last night in Nottingham where on Saturday there had been serious fighting in the streets around St Ann's Well area between white and coloured people.

The disturbances spread quickly and it was several hours before order was restored by the police. By then

dozens of men and women had been injured by bottles,
knives, razors and stakes. One man had to have 37
stitches in his throat and two others had more than a
dozen stitches each in wounds in the back.
MANCHESTER GUARDIAN AUGUST 25 1958

Taking one last look behind him, Andre slid hastily
through the door of number nine Blenheim Crescent.
The "Fortress".

The café at number nine was one of the few West
Indian owned businesses in the area. The welcoming
dwelling was owned by a Jamaican couple, Suzi and
Totobag. West Indians from all over London came to
hang out, play dominoes, and make new friends there.

It seemed only natural that in this hour of need, the
number nine would be the place for West Indians to
gather. In any case, reliable intelligence had informed
them that the "nigger-hunting" white gangs were that
night preparing an advance on number nine.

They had never attacked the building before, but
West Indians coming out of the building had been
assaulted and it seemed logical that they would take
great pleasure in torching this black-owned property.

About a hundred or so anxious West Indians and a
handful of white sympathisers had assembled in the
"Fortress". Most of Andre's friends were already there
— Webbie, Eddie, Byfield, Baker. He greeted them and
sat down. The emergency meeting had just
commenced and the atmosphere was tense.

Towards the centre of the gathering, Nancy, a fiery
Scottish woman, was zestfully stating her case. "Why

don't we just go out there and shoot them up. We can get the guns. That will be the end of it in one swoop."

Nancy angrily pushed aside her chair and stood up. "We've let these people get away with this for too long. Wiping them out is the only solution." She banged her fist down on the table.

"Calm down, girl," said Andre, ushering her to take a seat. "We have to be more rational about this situation. We have to act with our brains and think tactically."

"But where have tactics got us?" Nancy demanded.

"She could be right. I'm tired of this. I'm tired of not being able to walk the streets without the fear of attack." A voice from the back shouted.

Nancy sighed and sunk back in her seat. "I'm tired of hearing news of yet another coloured person getting beaten up. We know they are coming for us, so why don't we take this into our own hands?"

Her sentiments were approved by a chorus of nodding heads.

"Yes, I too agree," said Andre. "We are in a state of emergency and war. But we must think tactically. Yes, we do whatever is necessary to protect ourselves. But the ex-servicemen amongst you will know, the best way is through careful planning.

"Some of us may die tonight, but we'll do so with the satisfaction that we were fighting for survival."

Andre scanned around the room. These were life's survivors. Some of his other friends had already packed their bags and gone back to the Caribbean. Andre knew others who cried each night because they could not afford their passage back home.

He could understand them. The insult of being treated like this was almost too much. But Notting Hill was in a state of emergency and they had to respond to force with force to guarantee their own survival.

They were few in numbers, so they had to use skills and tactics to fight back. A couple of nights before, they had mounted a tripod on a van outside and placed a piece of wood on it and covered it with a blanket. Rumours quickly spread around that they had machine guns. This simple tactic proved effective and had the local police searching high and low for the weapon.

"Look, all ah you listen, here's what we going to do." Andre lowered his voice.

A sense of foreboding lurked in the deserted streets of Notting Hill. It was the quiet before the storm. A few stray locals scurried along, desperate to get home and not be drawn into that night's inevitable violence.

At number nine Blenheim Crescent, they were ready and keen to get the showdown over and done with. They might lose friends that night, but it was inevitable. After all, they were at war.

Armed with a batch of milk bottles stuffed with cloth doused in petrol, and a knife, Eddie and two others were stationed on the roof. Baker was posted to liaise with the police and throw them off the scent. Andre and Webbie made sure the Fortress was secure. Behind the drawn curtains, others were ready with an arsenal of sticks, iron bars, clubs and anything else they could lay their hands on.

Another group of West Indians were stationed a few miles away at the Blue Parrot café on the Harrow Road. They were the machete, meat cleaver, razor wielding crowd. If anything went wrong at the Fortress, the Blue Parrot posse were their back-up.

Apprehensive but aroused, they patiently waited for the pubs to shut and the riotous mob to take to the streets.

"They're on their way," a voice shouted from the roof, spotting the mob as they stormed into Blenheim Crescent hurling bricks. Some of the rioters were middle aged, but most in their late teens and early twenties. A few women trailed at the rear.

The gang halted outside number nine.

"Come out and fight. Show us what you're made off," yelled a skinny, scruffy blonde man who appeared to be the ring leader.

There was no response.

"Let's burn the niggers out," a voice shrieked to cheers. Then, as if on cue, a shower of Molotov cocktails rained down from the roof of number nine, as West Indians brandishing sticks tore out of the front door in hot pursuit of the startled white rioters.

But the police had been tipped off about the black/white showdown and dozens of Black Marias filled with officers sped into Blenheim Crescent, halting the imminent battle.

But Eddie could not contain himself, he jumped from the first floor window onto the pavement with a knife clenched between his teeth, vowing to claim his

In Fury

The mounting internal tension in battle-torn North Kensington in these past few days has never been paralleled before in its history. For several days and nights the rising numbers of arrests point to the seriousness and complications of the problem of the white man living in such uneasy proximity to the black.

As one resident of North Kensington put it this week: "Colour prejudice has been building up in N. Kensington for some time—perhaps at least two years. It doesn't restrict itself to people who are (or who allege to be) persecuted, but naturally soon spreads to relatives, friends and neighbours."

Conflicting opinions and statements have been voiced as to the cause of these riots. Some say it is originally the coloureds' fault with their habits of living and bad behaviour, and others point to possible disturbing influences brought onto the scene from outside. Others say it is sheer hooliganism.

Ugly scenes in which a vicious collection of weapons have been used are becoming horrible waking nightmares for coloured and white alike. Broken bottles, knives, sticks, chair and table legs, petrol bombs, chains, iron bars, whips and milk bottles are just some of the quickly fashioned instruments of these rash outbursts.

Almost 150 people have been arrested in the streets of North Kensington since the first night of disorder on Friday, 29th August.

Gangs (mostly white), large and small, have been roaming the dingy streets looking for trouble. The main areas of disturbances have been in Bramley Road, Latimer Road, Blechynden Street, Talbot Road, Ledbury Road, lower end of Clarendon Road, Portobello Road, and Blenheim Crescent.

'Housing Is Main Cause'
—Mr. Rogers

"LIMIT IMMIGRANTS" SUGGESTION

"The main cause of the trouble of the unrest in North Kensington is housing," said Mr. George Rogers M.P. for North Kensington, to "The Kensington News" on Thursday. "People are living in crowded houses, living cheek by jowl in vastly overcrowded conditions. To add to the difficulties some of the West Indians make no attempt to adapt themselves to the way of life here. Whilst I thoroughly deplore the riots and violence, naturally there is resentment that West Indians can buy houses here."

ACCOMMODATION AND EMPLOYMENT

On Wednesday he had gone to the Home Office to suggest courses of action to help solve the problem. First on his list was that there should be placed a restriction of entry on immigrants into overcrowded areas such as North Kensington. "Arrangements should be made," said Mr. Rogers, "that they be directed into proper accommodation and also attention should be given to the employment situation in those areas."

Second on his list was the suggestion to bring in legislation to enable the authorities to deport persons convicted of crimes of vice and violence.

INCREASED POWERS

revenge for the pain inflicted on the West Indians. He
was soon arrested.

*Nine youths who were sentenced to four years
imprisonment at the Old Bailey on Monday for
"hunting" coloured people in the Notting Hill area were
told by Mr Justice Salmon, 'It was you men who started
the whole of this violence in Notting Hill. You are a
minute and insignificant section of the population and
have brought shame upon that district in which you
live.' When the sentences were announced, there were
gasps and cries from the public gallery. Some women
had to be assisted out of court.*
KENSINGTON POST SEPTEMBER 19 1958

The night proved to be a turning point. The level of
violence against black people, although it did not
totally disappear, died down. The white gangs now
knew that their prey was prepared to fight back at any
cost.

As the questions began to be asked about the
events of the riotous fortnight in September, Andre
Shervington, Baron Baker and one or two others who
the police believed to be the black ringleaders were
charged with affray and summoned to Tower Bridge
Magistrates Court to account for their actions.

As soon as Crown Prosecutor Christopher
Humphries heard that Baker was being held in a cell,
he went to his assistance. The lawyer knew Baker
from his Colonial Office work.

"Why are you here?" he enquired.

"What am I doing here? You'd better tell them people to leave us alone, you hear?" answered Baker.

The Crown Prosecutor went upstairs and made arrangements for everyone of them to be released, except Gordon and Eddie, who had been arrested under more serious charges.

ABIDE WITH ME

Mr Norman Manley, the Chief Minister of Jamaica, and Dr Lacorbiniere, Deputy Prime Minister of the West Indies Federation, appealed for the Englishmen of 'influence and goodwill' to come forward and help solve the problems of race and colour in this country.

They made their appeals to a large and excited crowd of West Indians who had been called to hear their Ministers at Friends' House in Euston Road, London.

The appearance of the Ministers and Dr David Pitt, the prospective Labour candidate for Hampstead, and the Commissioner for the West Indies, Mr Garnet Gordon, aroused the twelve hundred black men and women in the hall to a frenzy of delight.

MANCHESTER GUARDIAN **8 SEPTEMBER 1958**

The tall distinguished white-headed figure of Jamaica's First Minister stood up and approached the platform. He nodded at the hordes of faithful West Indians who were waiting patiently to hear him speak.

Norman Manley cleared his voice, then began.

"I don't believe that the British public can tolerate this violence, I would not in Jamaica for five minutes." Manley paused effectively, then continued.

"I believe that evil forces are exploiting those West Indians in this country and . . . "

A delirious roar echoed around the room, halting Manley mid-sentence as the crowd signalled their immense approval.

The Minister held his hand up ushering the crowd to silence. He continued.

"The struggle for racial decency in the West is profoundly affected by these incidents. The coloured people in England are not the first to suffer this problem, their blood brothers in America have been suffering for a century.

"It is more tragic than Little Rock is for America. Anything in England which enables the leaders in Little Rock to boast and smirk is a disaster.

"I have come over from Jamaica to show you that you have a government that cares for you, to give you support and advice."

Most of the audience were now on their feet, uplifted and inspired by the sincerity of the Minister's words. Some loudly began chanting "Manley! Manley!" willing others to join them. Frustrated at looking over the tops of the heads of those who had had the foresight to arrive early, a handful manouvered themselves to the front, eager to get a closer look at the man with these powerful sentiments.

The Chief Minister once again jested for the crowd to quieten.

"You must at all costs have solidarity. You must not panic or be frightened of violence. They must not fail to exercise every single right that they had in this country. Above all you should be good citizens and seek to join the social and political life of this country.

"On the question of limiting immigration: It is a matter for the British Government, but we West Indians have greatly helped the cultural and economic life of this country. To change the open door policy would have a profound effect throughout the Commonwealth, and it would strike a fatal blow in the confidence that the world has in Great Britain."

When the jubilant cries for Norman Manley had finally subsided, local Labour MP George Rogers took to the platform.

"The solution to the colour problem is the introduction of legislation to enable the authorities to deport anyone convicted of crimes of vice and violence and also recruiting coloured police and detectives who can infiltrate black communities."

He could hardly be heard over the booing and hissing of the crowd. Renewed appeals for silence could not quell their disgust. Rogers pushed his heavy glasses up his nose and continued.

"I blame the British press for not giving enough space to the white point of view, every paper made out that all the whites were bad and all the blacks were angels.

"My white constituents in Notting Hill have legitimate grievances. Coloured landlords exploiting white tenants; coloured clubs which disturb the neighbourhood at night. Until there is better housing and better care of the coloured population, coloured immigration controls must be enforced."

The hall erupted into a venomous chorus of boos and cries for the MP to "get off". Some of the more incensed pushed to the front and angrily waved their fists up at the platform shouting: "We're British subjects, we have our rights."

Undeterred, but now barely audible above the raging din, Rogers shouted: "There is black discrimination against whites. Have you no criminals in the West Indies? I will make a bargain with you, you keep your criminals and we will keep ours."

Heckled by the enraged pack, the MP scurried off the stage. Dr Lacorbiniere hastily stepped in.

"The Honourable Minister is being ostrich-like. We will keep our criminals, but the West Indies Federation will never agree to, or condone, a limitation of coloured immigration. The root of the problem is colour and we must address that."

A large St Lucian woman seated near the front leaped to her feet and raucously applauded the Deputy Prime Minister's contribution.

"Our duty as civilised citizens is to demonstrate to those who do not understand that at least we understand how to be civilised," said Dr David Pitt. He begged the crowd not to meet evil with evil.

The large man paused to take a sip of water to cool himself in the stifling heat generating from the hall.

"We expect the authorities and the police to do their duty to stamp out violence, and that compensation be paid for the damage done to our property, but to penalise the victims of hooliganism by limiting

TEN AGAINST ONE

A number of youths—estimated at ten, are said to have attacked a coloured student in **Bramley Road**, North Kensington, last Wednesday night.

The young man, Ade Akinsanye, was walking to his Swinbrook Road, North Kensington, home when he was stopped by the youths. During the struggle he dropped his briefcase, containing law books, money and a Post Office savings book, and the gang made off with it.

Mr. Akinsanye was treated for a slight head wound.

immigration would be to bow to violence."

As Mr Manley left Friends House he was besieged by hordes of West Indians eager to speak to him. He graciously shook their hands. The eminent guests were then whisked off to another engagement.

Mr Manley and Dr Lacorbiniere expect to address another meeting in London later this week and they will visit Nottingham on Thursday. Yesterday morning they toured Notting Hill and Brixton. Mr Manley said that while in Notting Hill he felt even the children were hostile. In Brixton, he felt that there was a really integrated and happy society. Today they are to meet the Home Secretary and the Colonial Secretary and they also expect to see Mr Macmillan.
MANCHESTER GUARDIAN 8 SEPTEMBER 1958

The experience of that fortnight in the summer of 1958 forced many to return to the Caribbean. But Andre Shervington chose to stay. He would not let anyone push him out. After kissing his mother and father goodbye, he had never expected to go back under these circumstances.

For him these events just proved to people that the majority of West Indians were not going to turn and run, they were going to stay and fight.

Some looked towards the black power movement for an identity. Lots of do-gooders came to Notting Hill, many of whom saw the riots as a turning point in race relations.

But relations with the police continued to worsen. West Indians were beaten in police cells and the premises and houses of activists raided regularly. Andre had been arrested more times than he cared to remember. The current record was eight times in one night. He was often charged with obstructing police in the execution of their duties and breaching of the peace. Come night time, the police cells would be swollen to the brim with West Indians and Irish men.

They had to somehow get the police to respect them. So they organised marches and pickets to make Home Secretary R.A. Butler sit up and listen.

On Sundays over one hundred black people and white people would march from Hyde Park to Trafalgar Square, carrying banners that read, "Coloured men, women and children are suffering all forms of humiliation and oppression in the Mother country".

The relentless search goes on. Teams of determined detectives going round from house to house, asking questions, more questions and still more questions.

The area they search is as complex as it is large. Their task is monumental. They probe the houses of Notting Hill, Kensal Rise, North Kensington and Paddington.

They peer over bridges. They drag canals. The examine drains. They search dustbins.

The detectives with a tough task are looking for two things. A knife and a killer.

KENSINGTON NEWS 22 MAY 1959

A heavy silence reigned through the streets of Notting Hill. Today was a day of mourning.

A month ago, he was just another anonymous 'coloured' man. Now the name of Kelso Cochrane was on everyone's lips. The quiet 32-year-old Antiguan had been brutally stabbed to death. The motive, his colour.

Together black and white lined the streets to pay their respects. An endless procession trailed submissively behind the black hearse as it crept towards the Church of St Michael and All Angel. Male mourners wore dark tuxedos, women simply bore black cloth patches on their sleeves. Some shed tears, others were transfixed with anger at the heinous crime that had resulted in this senseless death.

Wreaths came from all sections of the black community, home and abroad. One had even come as far as Africa. Its red inscription read: "From the Martyrs and Victims of Oppression . . . Nyasaland."

Six tall West Indians slowly carried the coffin into the church, swiftly followed by the family who comfortingly huddled together.

Five hundred or more mourners managed to take their place in the church. Those who could not attend the service marched to Kensal Green cemetery. After a few verses of 'Abide With Me' most broke down in tears.

Coloured citizens of the United Kingdom, and possibly throughout the Commonwealth, have lost confidence in the ability of the law enforcing agencies to protect them.

This was the claim in a statement issued last night by the Committee for African Organisations. The Committee said that an emergency meeting in London of African and West Indian groups decided to send an open letter to the Prime Minister Harold Macmillan. It said:

'Our confidence is shaken. This crime rivals what we have seen or read about at Little Rock, or the recent lynching of Mr M.C. Parker of Popularville, Mississippi.'
MANCHESTER GUARDIAN MAY 19 1959

BEN'S STORY

**To the question who among the most famous they
would like to meet, Britain's teenagers, according
to the Sunday Times' poll, chose the Hon. Norman
Manley out of eleven personalities which included
Sir Winston Churchill, the Queen, Fidel Castro,
Elvis Presley and Sir Laurence Olivier. Why was
their choice of Jamaica's premier "somewhat
baffling" to the investigators? Is it too much to
suggest that perhaps it is because Britain's
teenagers are exploring their new relationship with
the New Britons?**
WEST INDIAN GAZETTE **DECEMBER 1959**

It was a crisp Sunday morning. The Pope regally
strolled down Portobello Road. A few yards away in the
middle of the footpath, he spotted an abandoned baby
wailing in a crib. He smiled and paused to bless the
child. As the Pope leaned over, he violently vomited
over the crying infant.

"Cut," yelled Frankie Y. "Ken that was great, but
maybe you can afford to be a little more exaggerated
with your vomiting. Let's go again."

"Scene three. Take two. Action."

Ben Bousquet shook his head. This was not what he had had in mind at all.

Two months ago his friend Frankie Y had invited him to write a script for a production. It was to be a ground-breaking effort featuring an all-black cast and production team, shot entirely on location amongst the bustle and market traders of Ladbroke Grove. Ken was to play the lead and Frankie had persuaded a few other professional actors to donate their time, free. As far as they knew it would be the first British all-black production.

Frankie Y was a member of the black power movement. Like his friend Michael X, inspired by recent events in America, he had taken on the yoke of the black British struggle.

Ben was on summer holidays from university and had been excited by the proposition. Making the film had been such fun, but now, nearing the end of production, it was clear the final version would be nothing like his original script.

He had painstakingly written about a young black man in Notting Hill trying to find himself, mentally and spiritually, but who was having a tough time adjusting to life in England. It was set against the background of the recent riots. You could say it was biographical of most of the black residents of north Kensington. But Frankie had changed everything.

"Frankie, are you sure this vomiting stuff will work?" Ben frowned.

"Yeah, man. It'll be great. Ben, you have to lighten up. This is what people want, none of that predictable fifties nonsense. The sixties is a whole new era for the moving image."

Ben gave in. He did not like what they were doing, but Frankie had a point, the avant-garde had paid north Kensington a visit and looked as if it was going to take up permanent residence.

Since the riots, a mystique had surrounded the W11 postal district. And word had got out about the transformation of the area. Journalists, celebrities and intellectuals made frequent visits, French writer Albert Camus and actor Sammy Davis Jnr could be seen sitting drinking continental style coffee and puffing on foreign cigarettes in cafés and bars that were once the sole domain of Teddy Boys.

Young intellectuals like Tariq Ali and Obi Ebgunu, who were beginning to make names for themselves in the student movement came and joined in the Notting Hill debate and some even became permanent residents.

Tory MP Mr Cyril Osbourne in a recent interview in the overseas DAILY GLEANER *accused the West Indian governments of refusing to place any control on their nationals who want to migrate to Britain.*

Said Mr Osbourne: 'We've got to stop the black flood engulfing England. We're building up fantastic problems for our grandchildren. They are going to curse us for not taking a strong line now.'
WEST INDIAN GAZETTE AUGUST 1960

The inter-racial tensions of the previous year had largely given way to a more integrated community. White, black, and Irish were now unified under the umbrella of Notting Hill. The residents had got together to better the plight of the local people as a whole. This was their community, if they did not start getting along soon, they would start killing each other again.

It would have been naive to assume all was well. Mosely still had a strong power base and continued to rally support. The police persisted in provoking and persecuting young black men. But the resilience of the black community during the riots had provided the impetus for action.

The People's Association was now a formalised multi-racial platform for the people of the north Kensington area to demand improvements in housing, play areas for the local children, rent controls and other issues. They had read about what was happening to black people in the United States and the hundreds and thousands oppressed under the apartheid regime in South Africa. They were determined that the plight of black people in England should not get that bad.

The fund to aid the St Lucia Babes, set up last November following news of the domestic tragedy when their 26-year-old mother was stabbed to death, which orphaned two adorable babies, Errol, eight months and

Leroy 32 months, now in care, began to pick up during the holidays.

Top of the list is Bedford, Bedfordshire. Due to the splendid initiative of a West Indian Gazette newsagent in that area, five pounds three shillings and six pence has been collected. The fund is to be made available for the children's needs, for their education and whatever immediate needs they may have.

WEST INDIAN GAZETTE JANUARY 1960

"How was it? You can tell me the truth?"

Ben heard an uncomfortable silence at the other end of the receiver.

"Well, to be totally honest with you, it was awful. Totally abysmal."

Let Death Be Your Santa Claus had premiered that night at the Classic cinema on King's Road, while Ben was conveniently tucked away in Cornwall hitch-hiking with his friend, Alf. His girlfriend had seen the film, but was none too impressed.

Yes, Ben had written it, but when the final production was finished he could not be persuaded to put his name to it. After all, what would his parents back home think if they knew he had made such a film. Instead Ben used the alias of Paul Dean. "Paul" because that was the name of his flat mate, and "Dean" after the rebel actor James Dean whose pouts and scowls were still driving young women into a frenzy long after his death in a car crash.

Ben vowed not to speak to Frankie for a very long time.

MARY'S STORY

Because she couldn't face going home a failure after four years in the United Kingdom, 30-year-old Ivy Thomas of Jamaica committed suicide in a Camberwell hostel for coloured girls.

At Coroner's Court, before Mr A Gordon Davies, the finding was that no foul play was involved. The "sensation-mad" papers' claims that she was engaged in a "ritual suicide" proved to be only guess work.

Mrs Mary Williams, the warden of Mostyn House told the coroner that Ivy was a 'skilled shorthand typist who wanted really to be a deaconess . . . ' But she felt she was thwarted on every hand. Uppermost in Ivy's mind was the thought that they were 'against my colour.'
WEST INDIAN GAZETTE **APRIL 1961**

If any of them was going to go, it was Mary. She was the most adventurous of her siblings. She was the one who rode the wild horses which wandered into the fields. She was the one who had bike races with the boys from the village, and beat them. She was the one who rounded up their father's cows when he was late coming home.

Joanne, Gloria, Joshua, Papie. They were all there to see Mary Johnson bid farewell to her home island of Antigua. All except Mommie.

She had said goodbye in her own special way back at Fig Tree Hall. She simply told her to be good and that they would meet again in God's hands. Mommie's 'goodbyes' suggested it was the last time she would see her daughter. Mary prayed it would not be.

She guessed it was because the only other time family had travelled so far was when her mother's father and brother went to Panama to work on the canal some years before. They both died of the plague there.

Looking at her remaining brother and sisters, it was hard for Mary to leave them. They all seemed so grown up now, especially Gloria. It seemed like yesterday when Mommie would dress them in the same frilly frocks and hair bows, as if they were twins.

Mommie was so fussy about them all being clean and presentable when in public. After all, they were the Johnson girls.

Mommie used to have their dresses and hats made. As far back as Mary could remember. She had thus insisted on dressing Mary and Gloria in identical outfits like twins, even though there was two years separating them.

Mary hated the way Mommie would scrape both their wayward Afros into two plaits and tightly tie ribbons around them.

Even when Mary's godmother in the States sent her

dresses, Mommie would always insist on getting similar dresses made for Gloria.

If Mommie was not around when they were getting ready for church, Mary would wear something different. Anything, as long as it was not the same as what Gloria had on.

Even Joshua was vain. With him everything matched. Mary remembered one particular outfit which featured a black and white tie, half black and half white. He had made such a big deal about it. He had really got on her nerves.

Mary used to say to them "render your heart and not your garment". After all, they were going to church.

But Joshua was the best brother anyone could have. He was always there for her. If they had ice cream or sweets, if he did not think there was enough to split four ways, he always let the girls have it.

Every Sunday before church they would get up and have a light breakfast, maybe some bun and cheese or toast and jelly.

Then the four of them, dressed in their best clothes, would walk the short two minute stroll along the dusty lane to church, a white two-storey old Methodist building, the focal point of the village.

The youngsters sat upstairs on the balcony while the adults occupied the wooden pews below. It gave the children a chance to whisper and have fun out of earshot of the adults. Occasionally, as the result of a dare, a piece of paper would go wafting down over the balcony. Everyone would quickly sit back so the suspicious eyes below could not identify the culprit.

If you were caught you would be in serious trouble. Mary remembered the time when Jane Williams' hat fell off. It was an accident but shocked the unsuspecting Miss Brown who was deeply engrossed in Minister Isaac's' sermon below. If Mary's memory served her correctly, Jane received a beating.

Sunday service always seemed to take for ever. First lesson, choir singing, second lesson, more choir singing and Minister Isaac would always have so much to say for himself. Mary's concentration would lapse somewhere between Luke chapter two, verse twenty six and Love thy neighbour, then would sharply revive towards the end when the Minister would slam his fists down violently on the pulpit — a ritual he would always perform, as if to make sure the congregation heard the final and most important message of the day's sermon.

Outside the church, after hastily exchanging the obligatory pleasantries about the sermon, it was back home for a proper breakfast. Spinach with salted cod fish, green bananas, fried dumplings and cassava, prepared early in the morning by the lady of the house.

Then after a couple of hours to digest their food, it was back to Sunday school for the children, to painstakingly recite passages from the Bible. To avoid any potential embarrassment in front of her peers, Mary always had hers learnt from the night before.

After Sunday school they went strolling. To nowhere in particular, maybe to the recreation park,

Church for the coloured gives help—to white people

BRIXTON'S first coloured pentecostal church, which holds regular services at the Gospel Hall in Sussex-rd., in the heart of the Jamaican community, is getting appeals for help from white people.

Several English families have visited the coloured founder-missionary, Miss Marcella White, at her home at Angell-rd., Brixton, after hearing that she distributes blankets and clothes to the needy.

She has never refused them.

Last Saturday she was distributing handbills, containing details of church services, in busy Brixton market when an English woman with two young children approached her for help.

OFFERING

"Come to the service tomorrow and we'll hold an offering for you," she promised.

The mother did so. After the service, Pastor Campbell, who is in charge, appealed to the congregation, mostly coloured. Several pounds was handed over to the woman.

Said Miss White, "Although we are primarily concerned in helping the Jamaicans who come to Britain, in many cases practically penniless, our church is open to anyone.

"Some white folk have joined our church and we are very glad to see or the beach. As they got older they went walking to rendezvous with boys. They would rush home, quickly adjust their hair and dresses, then meet up with friends before looking for the boys. Without parents knowing of course.

Mary's sister, Joanne, got in trouble once for talking to a boy named Clarence from St Paul's. Pappie gave her a "serious beating".

Mary had always loved going to church at Easter. "If you crack an egg in water on Good Friday, you can see into your future," Mommie used to say. As a child, Mary always wondered why she could never see anything. On Good Friday, most people would wear white, black or purple to church, the mood would be rather sombre. But then on Easter Sunday everyone would dress in new clothes and rejoice singing triumphant hymns.

As for school, Mary could not conjure up the same enthusiasm as she did for church. The regimental discipline and attention to detail bored her. Before school, the girls had to line up in the school yard and have their fingernails, hair and white shirts and blue pinafores inspected to make sure everyone was clean and presentable. Severe discipline awaited any girls who did not make the grade.

Miss Davies, the tall, bony teacher, was going on and on.

"Girls, cleanliness is next to Godliness," said the ageing coloured woman. "We are not just educating you but preparing you to be decent young ladies.

"Yvonne Baptiste, did you not press your uniform this morning? And your hands look grubby."

Mary kissed her teeth.

"Who did that?" Miss Davies spun round. Her eyes roamed over the girls suspiciously.

"I did," confessed Mary not wanting to get anyone else in trouble.

She was swiftly sent to the Headmistress who told her to apologise to the teacher in question for her rudeness.

Miss Davies was in the corner of the school, a huge wooden building where each class occupied a corner of the room

"Sorry." Mary spat out the word.

"Sorry whom?"

A few of the girls giggled.

Mary kissed her teeth again.

Miss Davies was a friend of her sister's godmother. She complained to her. When Mary heard what happened, she confronted her.

"She's not my mother. Don't go and complain to her about me." The matter was dropped.

It was at school that Mary had made up her mind that she wanted to go to England.

It was a Friday morning. Mary was sitting at the back of the class fanning herself with her book. She was bored. Miss Williamson's classes never really inspired her.

Her eyes roved around to the other classes to see if they were doing anything more interesting. That was

the benefit of the building, everyone was in the one
hall. Mary had heard that some of the newer schools
were being made with separate rooms for each class.
But that was a long way off for Saint Joseph's.

"Now, girls, I want you to write an essay about
where you want to be in the future. Title it, 'Me in the
year 1980'."

This interested Mary. She sat up and started to pay
attention.

"Just write about where you want to be, what you
want to be doing, who you want to be with. It can be
as outrageous or serious as you like," Miss Williamson
added.

1980 was a lifetime away, but Mary was pretty
clear about what she wanted. A good job, as a midwife
perhaps, because she had always loved babies. She
also wanted a husband and two children, and to
travel. She could not do that by staying on the island.

As the years went by the dream of going overseas
remained. The more Mary thought about the prospect,
the more attractive it seemed. Nothing exciting was
ever going to happen on the island. A runaway cow
was about as exciting as it got. England was as good
a place as any. Her friend Alice was there with her
mum and sister. She had written her and told her that
the hospitals in England needed workers.

Pappie was the most upset about Mary wanting to
leave for England. Endless tears rolled down his
smooth cheeks. Sixteen was far too young to be going
that far.

Mary had spent four months since she left school trying to persuade Pappie to let her go.

Pappie was very strict and adamant that his daughter could not go. He even promised to buy her a car to convince her to stay at home. It was tempting, few people had motor vehicles, Mary would be the envy of all of her friends. She fancied an Austin, metallic with varnished wood trimmings, or a Zephyr.

Mary could not be swayed. She eventually wore Pappie down by going on about it all the time. In most things she usually got what she wanted with him. Pappie finally gave his blessing for her to go and offered to pay the fare.

A baby was born to a 17-year-old British Guiana woman while on board the Grimaldi and Siosa Lines ship, 'Irpinia' bound for England. The baby, a girl, was named Antonia after the ship's Captain.
WEST INDIAN GAZETTE APRIL 1961

A few months later, here she was. Freshly pressed hair, pink cotton suit with a crushed velvet hat. Mrs Joseph had especially made the suit for her. Mary remembered being forced to sit through lectures on life in England, during all the fittings.

"You must be careful. There will be an abundance of temptation in England, but you must never give in to it. You come from a respectable home," the sprightly 73-year-old had warned.

Posters in the passport office in town had provided

a check list of things to do before going to England. Mary had a mental note of them ticked off in her head.

Make sure you have somewhere to stay.

She was going to stay with their close family friend Gigi.

Make sure you have a job.

She was going to work in a clothes factory until she could enrol in college.

Take warm clothes.

Pappie had bought this ugly old brown winter coat from Mr Murray. It was so old fashioned Mary planned to get rid of it the moment she arrived in England.

Take 20 pounds extra for train and bus fare.

Pappie had also taken care of that

Do not take more than your allowance of rum and cigarettes or you will incur a heavy fine.

Well, that really did not apply to her.

Her brown leather suitcase had been especially bought from Bryson's department store. Her brother had picked her some mangoes from the tree in the yard, there was also some patties from Granny.

Joshua placed his hands on her shoulders. "Set your own standard," he said, looking Mary straight in the eye.

An hour later. The BOAC plane screeched down the runway headed for London Airport. Mary was off on her adventure with life.

BLOODLINES

More than 174 amendments have been tabled by MPs, both Conservative and Labour, following the second reading of the colour-bar Commonwealth Immigrants Bill.

The measure seeks to restrict coloured Commonwealth citizens, particularly West Indians, Africans, Indians and Pakistanis from entry into the UK.

WEST INDIAN GAZETTE **DECEMBER 1961**

After a few years living and observing the English way of life, Connie Goodridge was beginning to develop her own views about how the West Indian immigrants interacted with the white indigenous people. It was okay for the black men to have white women, she concluded, but if black women had white men, then they were either whores or prostitutes.

"At the dance, if you are a coloured woman you stand there like a wallflower, the coloured men just ignore you and dance with all the white women," she wrote her cousin in Kingston.

Connie blamed it on the legacy of slavery, which

meant that it was now a big deal for black men to have white women. Like many West Indian women, she felt such relationships could not last. "The minute there was a fuss, the white woman would call the man a 'black bastard', and they'd go running back to their own people," she added in her long letter.

Well, if white men were out of bounds, there were plenty of black American GIs around from the air bases for Caribbean women to date. On Saturday afternoons in north Kensington, there would be a Yank on every corner with a bag full of liquor looking for some female company.

Like the day she met Joe.

Laden down with shopping, Connie was on the corner of Kensington High Street waiting for the number 137 bus to arrive. "Hi honey! Mmm, mmmn, mmm. You are so fine, honey child," a deep husky voice drawled at her.

A tall, handsome GI was holding his cap off to her. He had the kind of looks that could drive women wild — strong angular features, eyelashes that curled up at the ends, slick, shiny hair and a jet-black groomed moustache. But fine as he might have been, Connie was married.

"I'm all right, baby" she smiled "I can't talk to you right now, but I have a friend . . . She's a beautiful girl. You want to meet her?"

"Sure."

"Be here later. I'll come back."

The number 137 arrived and Connie hopped on.

"Myrtle, Myrtle you there!?" Connie shouted as she leapt up the stairs.

"Connie wha' you want?" Her friend wandered out of her room to see what the urgency was.

"Myrtle, me see a nice Yank, y' know. He so good-looking. Maybe we can have some fun tonight? Drinks, music . . ."

"Bring him home nuh, man," Myrtle ordered.

Connie rushed back to Kensington High Street and invited the Yank to come home with her.

Each week the man was different, but the scenario was the same. Sometimes Connie even brought back two Yanks! Her friends teased that she was a pimp for the lonely hearts.

This unconventional match-making also benefited Connie's social life. A house with a single woman and a Yank equalled a whole heap of Southern Comfort and partying.

There were so many single black women living in West Kensington, so they usually went from house to house. Come the weekend, if all her friends had dates, Connie and Stanley always found something else to do.

Stanley was an easy-going man. He made sure Connie had a break from the daily routine. She often took the Underground from Baron's Court to Piccadilly Circus and go to an American jazz club, buy a beer, have a cigarette, stay for a couple of hours and then go home.

As a woman out alone, men were always trying to pick her up. Connie's wit was always ready for them.

Sometimes on a Thursday she went to the Chiswick Empire to see a live act for a shilling. One night they even had a French striptease there. The doorman knew Connie's face and sometimes let her in free.

Stanley, on the other hand, found relaxation in visiting his brother in Leyton, east London and playing cricket.

Connie and Amru loved when the cricket season arrived. They would meet Stanley and travel around with the cricket team, exploring the whole of the country.

To the envy of her friends, Connie was also guaranteed tickets at Lord's Cricket Ground when the West Indies team was touring. Sometimes, when they were dying for some good old home cooking, the entire team would call on Connie to provide a big pot of rice-and-peas. It was the least she could do for them.

Cecil Holness had adapted to British life well. He was the secretary of the Anglo-Colonial Association that held monthly gatherings and social evenings. He would invite English people and West Indians down to come and talk, so they could get to know each other better.

A lot of the white people invited had not even spoken to West Indians before. Many had read in the press that black men could not talk, that they could not do this and could not do that, but few had ever come into close contact with a black man, so they remained ignorant. Some of them were in a position to employ black workers and, through the association, some did, because the white employers' attitudes were changing.

Most of the white people knew very little about the Caribbean. They knew it was where their sugar and rum came from, but nothing else. An Englishman even asked Cecil one day, "In what part of Jamaica would you find Trinidad?"

At the dances, sometimes there would be as much as sixty per cent white people. They liked the joyful calypso music and the vibrant colours the West Indians wore.

Some of Cecil's black friends were not so comfortable with his openness, complaining that he was being subservient to the white folk.

"I don't want to be subservient, but it's good if we can meet socially, because we have to work with them," he would reply.

Connie Goodridge flew upstairs towards the exit of the Underground station, almost knocking over a woman laden with shopping. It was too bad, Connie was running late.

Every day she would pick up Amru and Stanley Jnr at six o'clock on the dot from their child minder. The woman got so angry when she was even a couple of minutes late, and it was now quarter past. But it was not her fault, there had been a power failure on the

Underground.

Once above ground, Connie did a left down Munro Road and turned into Frances Street, nimbly dodging the rush hour rabble. It was now almost completely dark and starting to get foggy. She fished deep into her pocket for the piece of ribbon that she tied around Amru's hand so as not to lose her in the thick descending smog.

As she approached number thirty-eight, Connie stared in disbelief. 5-year-old Amru sat shivering on the kerb underneath the glare of a street light, while little Stanley's pram was a few yards away. He was crying.

"Mommy, Nanny said she could not wait as she had to take her daughter to ballet class," Amru blurted out, as she clutched her mother.

Connie's babies had been abandoned and left alone in the street.

Stanley Goodridge slowly climbed the stairs. Wary of losing his footing he clutched the wooden rail to guide him in the dark hall. The landlady saved money by not lighting the communal passageway. Funny, he thought, he would normally be near enough to chance a guess at what Connie had cooked for dinner. Maybe she was too tired to cook, he mused, feeling in his pocket for change to buy fish and chips.

When he reached the door to their bedsit, Stanley found Connie's key still in the latch and the door slightly ajar.

"Connie. Connie, baby, you there?"

The room was in total darkness, but he could hear a faint whimpering. He flicked on the light and saw Connie rocking backwards and forwards on the old green armchair clutching the baby. Her hands were so tight around him that Stanley could see the whites of her knuckles.

"Mommy's sick. She won't talk to me," cried Amru.

"Don't worry, baby, daddy's here now," Stanley reassured as he changed the baby's heavily soiled nappy.

Connie had finally been pushed over the edge. She was depressed. Depressed about living in England. Depressed about not finding anywhere decent to live. Depressed about only been given six weeks leave from work to stay with her new-born baby.

The Goodridges had several Caribbean friends who were as sharp as needles one day, then in a lazy, vegetative state the next, unable to feed or wash themselves properly. Connie knew the illness was England. It was contagious, but she was adamant that it would never get hold of her. But her will had worn thin.

The doctor prescribed tablets and rest. During the day she had to take more pills to keep her awake. Connie became addicted to the tablets which worsened her state of mind. Going home was the only cure. Connie handed in her notice at the hospital, booked two one-way tickets to Jamaica and sent a telegram notifying the family of her imminent arrival.

"Promise you'll join us in a couple of months when you've tied up things here."

"Yes, of course I will. I can't go without seeing my family for so long," replied Stanley.

Connie hugged her husband for a final time. Her eyes were filled with tears, just like when Stanley had left her to first come to England. Even though that day now seemed almost a lifetime ago, the pain of being apart from her husband was still vivid.

But nothing could dampen the relief she felt as she climbed the long steps and boarded the BOAC flight to Jamaica. At last, she was on her way home.

"Amru, cheer up. You're going to love Jamaica. You'll have so much space to play."

Stanley Jnr slept as soon as he was comfortably positioned on Connie's lap. But Amru was restless. She fidgeted and stamped her feet, restrained by the seat belt and confined space.

"You can go to the beach everyday, pick fruit from the trees and you'll have all of your cousins to play with," Connie tempted.

"But Mommy, why did we have to leave daddy?" Amru asked innocently.

Connie didn't have an answer but continued trying to convince her daughter of how great Jamaica would be. She had so many of her own childhood memories to share with her.

As a child, Connie had loved music. Five o'clock every Saturday morning, without fail, she would leap out of bed and go to piano classes at Kathleen Bond's house. Come examination time, all of the class passed with distinctions or merits. The teacher was so proud of her pupils, she had made a plaque engraved with all their names, and put it up in the studio.

Although Connie also excelled at school, she did not have the same enthusiasm and spent most of her time chatting to her friends.

"Constance MacDonald take an order mark for talking" her five foot tall art teacher would always say.

"You doing art and drawing, what else is there to do but talk?" Connie mumbled to herself.

After Saturday morning piano class they would go walking on King Street in the centre of Kingston, parading up and down. The girls tried to appear pretty and sophisticated in their school gymslips and white blouses that they wore every day, even on a Saturday, whilst boys would stand and watch them. It was a big deal if any of them spoke to Connie or her friends, especially if the boys were at high school.

Connie also liked to sing. Her and her father formed a group with Mr and Mrs Nelson. Mr Nelson sang bass, Connie's father was tenor, she was alto and Mrs Nelson the soprano. They used to get invited to churches all over Jamaica to sing.

On Sunday evenings, her family would hold concerts at home. Connie's father was chairman and insisted on everyone contributing a performance. Aunts and uncles and cousins were invited, but each had to perform a recital or a song. Even the youngest member of the family, Connie's 2-year-old cousin, had to do something. He would stumble on the make-shift stage and say "Jesus wept," then bow and come off. Then everyone would clap. It was the shortest verse in the Bible, the only verse he could manage.

Although Connie lived in town, because her father was from the country he made sure she learned about the rural way of life. Every morning Connie would suck a raw egg and run a mile before she went to school. Her father believed in exercise. He never took a bus, and rode his bicycle or walked everywhere. Sometimes Connie would complain about not having the luxury of a car, particularly when she saw her neighbours ostentatiously driving around town: "The higher a monkey climbs the more of his backside you see," her mother would say.

Connie's dad taught her how to ride on his old black bicycle. When she first tried to ride it, Connie's feet could not reach the ground, now she was able to steer with her feet.

At the weekends, Connie's mother would cook up a lot of fish and hard-dough bread and they would go for long walks. Connie's father would put her on his back and cross over the river.

In her teen years, Connie spent most of her spare time going to the beach with her girl friends. They wore a different bikini each time. A friend who was good at sewing would make them quite easily, but their parents would object to the itsybitsy styles: "Too much flesh show," Connie's father would say, so she would wear trousers over her bikini briefs until they got around the corner and then took them off. She made sure to put them back on before she got home.

Hundreds of English, West Indians, Africans, Indians, Pakistanis, Irish, Scots, Welsh, Cypriots and others, will join a protest march and demonstration against the Commonwealth Immigrants Bill. Called by the Movement for Colonial Freedom for mid-January, the demonstration marks a high point in its campaign against the Bill. The march is also in support of Mr Fenner Brockway's Bill making racial and religious discrimination illegal.

WEST INDIAN GAZETTE JANUARY 1962

The raging Kingston sun overwhelmed Connie as she descended from the plane onto the scorching tarmac. Connie had not realised how much she had missed home. Her senses were instantly revived by the smog-free air.

"Phew! It hot man," she grinned. "See how the sun shine in ah Jamaica, Amru. England says it has summer, it ain't nothing compared to the Caribbean sun. Look, see your family has come to meet you." Connie pointed at the crowd of smiling faces behind the barriers.

It was like the return of the prodigal daughter. The Goodridge and MacDonald family were all there to welcome Connie back into the fold. But it was the grandchildren who were the real focus of attention. At least their presence would delay the impending interrogation from her mother-in-law.

From what Connie had heard, her family had taken most of her belongings in Jamaica for themselves. "Me gwine tek it, she nuh come back," they had said.

When she arrived at her house, it was true. The building was virtually empty and in need of repair. But it would take much more than that to put her off. She was a determined woman.

Even though she had been away for such a long time, it did not take Connie long to ease back into the Jamaican groove. After a phone call or two, she got her job back at University College Hospital as a medical secretary and bought back her furniture. And once word was out that Connie Goodridge was back in town, her social calendar blossomed. Within a couple of weeks, the thin lines of worry vanished, her hair recaptured its glossy sheen and her figure plumped out to more shapely proportions; Connie looked and felt twenty years younger.

INDEPENDENCE DAY

"Charlie, Charlie, turn dat music down, bwoy. Why you have to play dat noise so loud?"

"Charlie! You hear what your mother say, bwoy?"

Charlie Phillips sighed. The dulcet big band sound of his classic 1930s Louis Jordan sounded so good, it would be a crime to even try to restrain it. In any case, this was his turn on the Bluespot gram.

Every Sunday morning, while Charlie was sleeping off the effects of heavy partying the night before, he would receive a rude awakening as Jim Reeves and Nat King Cole crooned their way through the narrow gap underneath his bedroom door. Late Saturday night, once his parents had gone to bed, 16-year-old Charlie would sneak out of the house and go to the local blues dances on Talbot Road or Latimer Road. Sometimes he would even venture as far as Somerleyton Road in Brixton. So far he had not been caught. His parents slept too soundly for that.

He never complained about his parents' early morning ritual. He conceded that the Bluespot was their property.

The knee-high, highly polished, imitation teak cabinet, built with a "bass that could kill", had pride of place in the centre of the Phillips' tiny main room. After a bed, it was the second item they had saved to buy when they arrived in England. In terms of its monetary value, it was a luxurious item to purchase. A British company had come out with what they thought was a cheaper alternative called Dynatron, but nothing could test this German-made model. It was like a mortal sin for any self-respecting Jamaican household not to have a Bluespot.

Like a member of the family, the Bluespot was well looked after. Every other day, Charlie's mother would painstakingly clean it. First she would clear its top of the plastic decorative ornaments brought from home, then, one by one, she would take the miniature glasses (that were always ready for those special occasions when someone dropped in with a gift of Wray and Nephew rum) from the shelves. Lastly, she'd lovingly rub the wood with methylated spirits, then slowly put everything back in its place.

As well as their Sunday morning session, Charlie's parents also had a seven o'clock booking with the Bluespot. They would punch the magic dial to tune into Radio Luxembourg for rhythm and blues with a hint of rock and roll, provided by the likes of Fats Domino, The Drifters or Little Richard. At eleven it was time for Willis Conniver, the Voice of America, and the magic dial was tuned so Charlie could listen to the be-bop sounds of Messrs Gillespie and Parker.

Although Charlie had a passion for jazz and wanted to be a conductor, he was also a keen photographer. One of his relatives had bought him a Brownie camera. It was far too expensive to send the negatives away to be developed so Charlie had no alternative but to learn to develop them himself.

The man at the chemist round the corner mixed up some chemicals and with a red bulb and a few sheets, the bathroom became his dark room. The first attempts were disastrous. But eventually after much trial and a lot of error, Charlie got the hang of it and started to develop good postcard size prints.

He took pictures of everything he came across to hone his new found skill. Strangers in the street, objects around the house, friends at play, they all fell under the scrutiny of Charlie's lens.

His parents thought he was crazy. One day they even banned him from taking any more pictures. Fixer had dripped onto the bathroom lino leaving an immovable muddy brown stain. But after the anger had subsided and the stinging pain of the 'licks' he was given lessened, Charlie was back at work.

"Charlie, you hear me boy? Turn that music down. Now!"

"Okay, okay. I hear you."

Her Majesty The Queen of England sends today to Jamaica her Royal sister the Princess Margaret to grace the ceremonies which will mark Jamaica's independence.

It was under another Queen of England, over a century ago that the children of Africa in Jamaica were relieved of bondage to other men. Thus was shame removed from owner and owned so that pride as a people could begin to grow.

Now Victoria's modern heir Elizabeth II of England becomes the Queen of Independence. Long may she reign as titular head of our young nation.
DAILY GLEANER AUGUST 3 1962

On the twelfth stroke of midnight the red, white and blue of the British Empire slipped down the tall white pole. The Union Jack was now destined to become a quaint remnant of the past. As the green, black and gold of the future was hoist high into the sky, Jamaica began to rejoice the birth of her new era.

"Jamaica, Jamaica, Jamaica. Land we love," voices across the island passionately sung out, pledging their fidelity to this new nation. A kaleidoscope of fireworks exploded into the night and bonfires raged on the peaks of the hills. All over Jamaica, months of preparation was coming into fruition.

In Port Antonio, green, gold and black streamers and balloons had been entwined around public buildings. In Montego Bay arches of hope made from bamboo had been positioned across streets. In Kingston, shops had offered Independence Day discounts. In the country, villagers donated their own money to make sure their independence festivities would not be outdone by those of the towns. Fish had been fried, meat seasoned, limes squeezed, fruits soaked, steel bands booked, costumes made, hair appointments scheduled and balls were organised.

That night, Connie Goodridge joined other Kingstonians and jumped up in King Street to the Sugar Belly orchestra which saw feuding enemies dancing up like long time friends, grandmothers jerking their hips with the youths and high-yellow bank clerks sharing drinks with ebony-coloured road sweepers. The parties promised to go on for the next few days as Jamaica rejoiced in its freedom.

Five thousand hand flags have been flown from the West Indies to Britain for distribution to Jamaican students, nurses and schoolchildren.

The British celebrations which have already begun include dinners, tea and cocktail parties, civic receptions, dances, parades and processions. They will be held not only in London, but in Coventry, Manchester, Birmingham, Leeds and Sheffield.
DAILY GLEANER AUGUST 3 1962

"We're free! We're free!" Charlie Phillips joined in the jubilant chants emanating from the crammed hall. With his parents and about a hundred or so other Jamaicans he had boarded a coach bound for a huge blues dance in Wolverhampton to celebrate their island's coming of age. Though far from home, they were determined that Independence Day would not go uncelebrated.

The DJs squawked eulogistically between the records praising "God Almighty" for delivering Jamaica to independence. They spun the latest sounds from men like Duke Reid and Prince Buster who were pioneering a new musical movement back home, some called this blend of be-bop, soul and

African sounds Kingstonian ghetto music, some called it ska or blue beat. Whatever it was called, it symbolised the spirit of change that was sweeping across Jamaica.

Charlie helped himself to another Russian Stingo Stout. Youths younger than himself were also indulging in the vast array of liquor on offer. As for the adults, they were all too inebriated and ecstatic to care. There were stacks of plastic crates filled with bottles of Stingo Stout between the rows and rows of Wray and Nephew rum. But the drink had loosened tongues.

"Me seh now Jamaica free de country will ruin."

"Cha man, how you seh dat? Bustamante 'ave it all under control. He ah run t'ings now."

"Me know he is a leader, but me seh him gwine have problems."

These words of cynicism were quickly drowned out by the euphoria of emancipation.

IO'S STORY

President Kennedy was assassinated yesterday in Dallas, Texas, three shots were fired as the President's open car passed an intersection in the main business area of the city.

He was hit in the head and died in hospital soon afterwards. Vice President Lyndon Baines Johnson has been sworn in as the new President.
THE TIMES NOVEMBER 23 1963

The Virgin Mary in all her splendour gazed down lovingly on the congregation. Pastor Francis had had a dream and today that dream had come true.

For months the congregation had been meeting in the front room of his terraced house in Clapton. It had started off with a handful of men and women. Then the congregation began to grow. When there were not enough seats to go round, people brought their own. As the numbers continued to grow, the tables and chairs were pushed aside to make more standing room.

Then one night Pastor Francis had a vision of a hall at the end of a road, with a white man standing inside.

A few weeks later the congregation was offered a room at St Barnabas' Church in Homerton High Street by a white caretaker. Although it was the smallest, dirtiest hall in the building, with broken furniture and no heating, Io Smith smiled to herself, she knew this was a beginning of better things to come.

Io was not particularly religious back home in Jamaica, she was a Christian and had faith, but it was more of a tradition than a commitment. But the life she had met in Britain drove her to pray more and develop a closer bond with God. She felt she was not equipped to handle life without a strong faith.

Io had come to London to be with her childhood sweetheart, Len. Her father was a scout master back in Jamaica, and Len had been a member of his group. Those early scout meetings were held at her home, so Len would always be at their house at weekends.

They walked together, ate together, played together. In the end, they did not realise that they were falling in love until it was past the point of no return.

Io could not figure out why their relationship caused a terrible upset in her family. She guessed it was because her father felt she could not cope with marriage at seventeen. The situation created a lot of tension in both households and various attempts were made to keep the couple apart. As a last resort, Len was packed off to Britain. His family hoped the distance would finish the relationship, but they were wrong.

Unknown to their parents, Len intended to work

and earn enough money to pay for Io's fare to England. She not only wanted to join Len but, by going to England, she also felt she was improving her education. Io knew of many people who had left Jamaica for England. A couple of families in her village sold their land and cattle so they could send their children. There was already a hierarchy developing by people who had studied in England and returned to Jamaica and Io wanted to be a part of it.

What Io found in Britain was overt racism and prejudice and, because she could not find it anywhere else, she sought solace in the guise of Christianity and the church. But she was wrong.

At the first place of worship she went to everyone stared at her as if she was from Mars. After the service, she had waited patiently to shake the minister's hand. He held onto the hand of the lady in front of Io for ages, waiting for the black woman to give up.

In the next church she visited, a lady said to her, "Did you hear what the minister said to you? He said, "Don't make your visits too often, or you'll scare the congregation away." Another Minster told her, "I think the church down the road wants coloured people." In other churches, she was simply ignored.

Through her perseverance and a little bit of divine luck, Io eventually found a place of worship. She had gone to the market, not to shop but to meet people.

There a woman invited her to a prayer meeting in a bedsit in a house near Roman Road in the East End. There were only two other people there, but the sense of unity and welcome prevailed.

Then a woman invited Io and Len to a church being run by a group of black people in north London. They all crowded into the front room of a house on the Holloway Road. Io had found her freedom and sense of belonging.

These joyous celebrations were so infectious that sometimes Io would arrive at the house on Sunday morning and not go home until that evening.

Io was then fortunate enough to be invited to a prayer meeting in Clapton where Pastor Francis and his wife, Julia, lived in their humble terraced house cum place of Pentecostal worship.

WINSTON'S STORY

The shiny red number 68 double decker bus screeched to a sudden halt. Its conductor Winston Stafford-Husband stepped off the bus on to the pavement to see what was happening.

Just a few yards away, a large, fairly attractive white woman was walking proudly down the busy Camden High Street, "naked as she was born". Only a few strands of her bright auburn hair strategically concealed her breasts.

Unsuspecting drivers had been carelessly distracted by the strange but satisfying sight of this naked lady striding boldly between puzzled shoppers. With their drivers' attention drawn from the road, vehicles piled helplessly into one another.

As tempers flared over their vehicles' damaged fenders and the resulting traffic gridlock, the police arrived swiftly on the scene. Within minutes they had shifted the mangled iron mess and stopped this would-be Lady Godiva from taking any more victims.

Winston sniggered to himself. "And they said England was a civilised country!"

He was settling to life as a London Transport bus conductor quite comfortably. He worked on the 68 bus route from the leafy suburb of Croydon to bustling Chalk Farm.

London Transport had offered him all that he was looking for. His mother had told him that he could not leave home until he was at least twenty-one. This would mean he would have had to have waited several more years. But after reasoning with his father, he was allowed to leave with friends on a plane bound for England.

His fare from Barbados to England was paid by his prospective employers. A minimal sum was then deducted from his salary each month until he had reimbursed the company. Through London Transport Winston also found somewhere to live with relative ease, a house in New Cross, south east London which he shared with five other West Indians who had come to work on the buses.

Winston had spent nearly a fortnight training at the London Transport centre in Chiswick, west London, then a week shadowing a conductor on the bus. He was then left to work on his own. Fortunately he was attached to a West Indian driver, who patiently showed him the ropes. The money was no problem either, it was the same pound shillings and pence he had learned as a child at school back home.

But he did have to deal with the one or two passengers who refused to part with threepence for the journey. Depending on their size, Winston had two ways of dealing with this situation. For children, women and men who were under five foot seven, he would confidently stand his ground and order them to pay, or get off the bus. But for the others, Winston would let it ride.

There were perks with the job too. As a conductor he had the perfect opportunity to introduce himself to pretty girls who would ride the bus. He could also see most of London's tourist sights courtesy of his employer. After work, there was so many activities to choose from — cricket, table tennis, snooker. Employees could even learn how to fly a plane if they so wished. The camaraderie that he had found within London Transport was a powerful bonding force, and pulled him through those initial hostile months in Britain.

Winston fancied himself as a driver. One day he went up to the centre in Chiswick to test drive a simulated bus. But nerves got the better of him and it was a disaster. He knocked down all the 'virtual' houses and drove the bus all over the 'virtual' park. The instructor told him that he would never make a driver.

Winston took his dented ego and sat his car driving test. He passed first time.

'MIXED' DANCE
IS A SUCCESS
IN LAMBETH

NOW it is proved that Lambeth's coloured and white folk can mix socially, the borough's Anglo-West Indian committee will probably adopt the theme of " Co-existence through calypsos and Cockney cabaret."

The colour bar, if any, was completely broken down on Friday at the Assembly Hall in Acre-lane.

Inside, 180 West Indians taught 180 natives of Lambeth their version of mambas, sambas rhumbas.

The dark-skinned guests hung back as an English band broke into a fox-trot. At first white danced with white, coloured with coloured.

Then came the Sunset-Serenaders, a West Indian band —and things livened up.

Coloured guests piloted the wives of councillors to the floor and Leon Goldrich, a Lambeth Walk salesman, grabbed a lithe coloured nurse for a vigorous jive session.

M.P.s, councillors and aldermen followed suit, and the Mayor, as chairman of the committee which sponsored the affair, partnered 22-year-old King's College student, Pamela Nichols from Trinidad.

Two Brixton girls, Pauline Stanley (16), and Joan Stephens (13), in Pearly attire, showed the " Lambeth Walk " and " Knees Up Mother Brown," which they had been practising for a week.

Then it was the West Indians' turn in a cabaret of singers, crooner and acrobats and the Trinidad steel band whose "instruments" were oil drums.

The steel band music (akin to an electric organ) held the audience entranced. " Somebody Bad Stole De Wedding Bell," and it was one of the highspots of the evening.

Newsreel cameras were whirring, and the film will be shown from Thursday at ABC, Regals and other cinemas including Brixton Palladium.

The Anglo-West Indian Committee financed the dance out of their funds and a £17 collection

WINDS OF CHANGE

27-year-old Astley Lloyd Blake of Jamaica became the first coloured police constable to be appointed in Britain on January 31st.

Taking the oath of allegiance at Gloucester, he was welcomed by the chairman of the Magistrates, who told him: 'I am sure you will be a great help to me.'

The case for appointing coloured police has long been raised. Recently an officer of the Standing Conference of West Indian Organisations again made suggestions along those lines.

WEST INDIAN GAZETTE MARCH 1964

"Come on Mary. We're going to be late."

"Yes, but I'm running as fast as I can in this skirt. I don't want to rip it. It took ages to make."

"But Mary, if Matron catches us coming in late again, Lord knows what she will do," sighed Jean.

The pair had missed the ten o' clock curfew that all the student nurses had to abide by. Like most Friday nights when they were not on duty, they had gone to see a movie. But the curfew never allowed enough time for the walk back.

Matron was a fierce-looking Scottish woman with brilliant red hair. The nurses swore she had special powers that made her able to detect them from one hundred miles away. If the nurses were caught they were forced to endure a stiff lecture the following morning in matron's office, and a week's grounding.

Mary steered Jean towards the back of the building.

"Come, let's climb over the wall. I'm sure it leads to the fire door in the study hall," suggested Mary.

"Okay. You could be right."

The girls scaled the wall. They were just about to jump to the ground on the other side when Jean's coat slipped out of her hands and dropped into the blackness below. It was a long drop.

"Mary. Maybe this is not such a good idea. I don't think we're going to make it if we jump."

"Yeah, maybe we should just go and face the music."

Hesitantly Mary and Jean crept threw the main entrance.

"Nurses Johnson and Thomas. Come here at once." They had been caught.

Mary Johnson was having such a great time in London. When she first arrived, she had stayed with Gigi, a family friend in Battersea. She had been too young to start training as a nurse, so went to work in a factory with Gigi's younger daughter. She was put in charge of a machine that took the raw edge off cloth.

It was easy, once they got the hang of it. Any mistakes made were mainly due to her chatting instead of concentrating on her work.

When she was eighteen Mary was accepted at Bolingbrook Hospital in Battersea to do her State Registered Nurses course. Her main duties were making beds, assisting the Staff nurses, and dressing wounds. Like the other trainees, Mary only received nine pounds a month, but her accommodation and meals were paid for.

At the nurses' home, Mary shared a basic double room with a cupboard and desk. The bath and toilet were at the end of the corridor. The bland meals mainly consisted of Irish stew or a liver, bacon and sausage fry-up.

But Mary thrived on her life at the nurses home, the residents were like sisters. Together they laughed, played, consoled each other, shared secrets, argued, even fought. They were like one big happy family, with one of the African nurses, Barbara, as the mother-figure. She was married, with children, but her family was in Nigeria, so she lived at the nurses home with her younger colleagues.

Although they had a similar history and background, Mary found that on the whole, West Indians in England viewed Africans with suspicion and distaste. They did not like the way they spoke, what they cooked and the way they dressed — ironically, the same things that English people disliked about the West Indians.

Barbara supplied her wide-eyed young companions with a more worldly education. Thursdays she would get dressed up in her fanciest clothes and announce she was going out with her Uncle. Barbara would then disappear into a slick black Zephyr waiting outside. Hours later, she would return bearing gifts of expensive brandy, chocolates and French perfume. It was weeks before they wised up to the true nature of Barbara's Thursday liaison with her "Uncle".

Two days after pay day, most of Mary's money was gone. But if one of them had money, all of them had money. They would go to the local cinema to swoon over Tony Curtis, Sidney Poitier or Rock Hudson, or go ice skating at the rink in Streatham, or to Battersea Pleasure Gardens and fun fair to ride on the neon-coloured merry-go-rounds. At the weekend, they would get glammed up and party all night, then go straight to work the next morning.

Though by December, this sisterly affinity Mary had found in England could not make up for the absence of her true family. It was a time of immense homesickness.

The comforting scent of baking bread blended with roasting honey-coated ham wafted out of the kitchen, arousing Mary's adolescent taste buds. In search of a sneak preview of her mother's legendary Christmas goodies, Mary would tussle with her siblings to suck the thick, sweet cake mixture off the wooden spoon.

She did not care much for spending too much time helping with the culinary preparations. Her contribution to the occasion was the slaying of the sacrificial Christmas chicken. Armed with a meat cleaver, Mary would roam the yard, in search of the slowest, plumpest bird, then with one deft swoop, its fate would be sealed. She would leave the mundane task of plucking the feathers to her squeamish sisters.

On Christmas Eve, the family would gather together and decorate the house with red balloons, multi-coloured streamers and cherry tree branches adorned with yellow and red paper bells.

After breakfast on Christmas morning amidst the idle banter and boasts of what presents they had received, Mary and her sisters would listen out for the call of the Jug Band. Their hollow melodic chant created with industrial pipes and bottles could be heard for miles, and was the signal for children to rustle up Christmas treats for the innovative entertainers — some cake or a drink of wine perhaps.

Then at one o'clock, the lady of the house rounded up the Johnson clan for Christmas dinner. Salami, chicken, rice, peas, potatoes, macaroni cheese, home-made guava ice cream, black cake, all washed down with sorrel or ginger beer.

On this first Christmas in England, Mary had to be content with sending a card wishing her family seasons best wishes. To ease the pain of being so far from home, she volunteered to work during this season of festivities, entertaining patients who were unlucky enough to be in hospital over this period.

The eve before Christmas, they turned their nursing capes on the reverse red side and went carol singing on the wards. Then on the day itself they handed out drinks, stout for the men and wine for the women. Between rounds they would take a sip for themselves. One Christmas, Mary took too many sips and ended up spending Christmas night in the nurses' room watching television upside down.

Nobody quite believes it yet. That is, nobody who is anybody. But Cassius Clay did defeat the 'unbeatable' Sonny Liston, and is World Heavyweight Champion. The lad not only talked but fought.
WEST INDIAN GAZETTE MARCH 1964

The mint green Ford Consul was parked provocatively outside the house. From the window of his room, Norman Phillips eyed the car longingly. It was so tempting to take it for a spin. But there was one small factor to consider. He could not drive.

He sighed and flicked on the television. He had rented the 17 inch black and white for a ten day trial from the rental shop in town. That was three weeks ago. He had moved since then and the rental company did not have a record of his new address. Eventually Norman would sell the set and make some good money. He had done exactly the same thing many times before. Televisions were a luxury and people wanted them.

Norman got up again and looked at the Consul. How difficult could it be to drive? He decided to find out.

Easing himself into the plastic imitation leather seat, he fiddled, pushed and twisted the levers on the wooden dashboard, but had no idea what to do next.

After a few minutes of more fiddling, pushing and twisting, Norman ran back in the house to telephone for help.

"Harry. Help me, nuh man. How you start this car? I wanna take it for a spin."

"You just put the key in the ignition and push a button."

"Me know that. But where is the ignition?"

"You nuh know?" Harry laughed. "It should be to the left of the steering wheel."

"Oh okay, I see."

"Norman, why you want to drive a car if you nuh know where to put the key?"

"Don't worry, I have it sorted." Norman smiled and put down the receiver.

Fuelled with confidence, he got back into the Consul and put the key in the ignition. The engine roared as he pumped the accelerator. Norman switched the ignition off and on a couple of times then, charged with adrenaline, he was ready to make a move.

From observing seasoned drivers he was clear about the basis of driving: Clutch. First gear. Hand brake off. Accelerate. Slowly Norman went through each stage. The car jolted forwards and the engine cut out. He sighed then started again. Clutch. First gear. Hand break off. Accelerate. Hesitantly the Consul edged forwards.

Locked in first gear, the Consul rolled slowly down the street, drifting dangerously near parked cars. Its driver clutched the steering wheel with impenetrable concentration.

In time Norman had almost driven around in full a circle. But to get home again he would have to drive up Roseberry Hill. As he approached the traffic lights at the top of the steep road, Norman pleaded with them to stay green. He pumped on the accelerator to make the car go a little faster, but the vehicle strained and stuttered in first gear.

Just as he reached the lights, they switched to amber, then red. Norman put the handbrake on, slipped into neutral and waited nervously for his first hill start. The lights changed to green. He slipped into first gear, then took the hand brake off. The car rolled backwards. He tried it again. The same thing happened. The lights changed back to red. Panicked and cursing, Norman stalled the car. Impatient drivers behind began to honk their horns and hurl abuses.

Alerted to what was going on, a handful of passers-by came to the novice driver's rescue by wedging rocks behind his rear wheels. As the lights changed, Norman slammed his foot hard on the accelerator and furiously sped off home. That afternoon he went to the driving school and booked up a course of lessons.

Claude was really to blame for this impulsive test drive. Norman had moved to the north of England to work, as there were more opportunities than in London. Through shifts as a labourer in the steel yards or coal mines he could save some cash.

He had found cheap accommodation in Bradford, but Norman felt trapped and isolated in this sleepy rural town. Neighbouring Leeds was much more lively, but it was some distance away. Norman saw a car for two hundred and fifty pounds so he put down a deposit of forty pounds then agreed to pay a fixed amount per month. He still did not have a driving licence but his friend Claude did, so they came to an arrangement.

But it did not work out quite as Norman planned. Every time he wanted to go somewhere, Claude had the car and was nowhere to be found. Sometimes Norman was lucky if he brought the car back that week. He also suspected his friend used the car to impress women.

Eventually, Norman had had enough and told Claude to leave the car and only drive it when he was with him. Claude got vexed and threw the keys at Norman. It was then that Norman took the initiative to get a licence.

It was eight o'clock in the morning. Norman, Claude and Joe were returning from a party in Sheffield. Claude had apologised for his outburst and was back driving the Consul along the narrow country lane.

"Come, let me drive."

Claude turned and looked at Norman. "No, no I can't give you a trial. Anything can happen and I want to get home."

"Come outta me car, man. You see that long road down there, I'm going to drive down and turn around."

"You can't drive. If by a miracle you succeed I promise to drive your car for you any day you want."

Norman woke Joe who was blissfully sleeping in

the back and ushered both men out of the car.

"I was sleeping, why you put me in the cold? What's going on?" Joe asked, feeling aggrieved.

Claude shrugged his shoulders. "Maybe Norman's gone mad."

Norman slammed the car door and sped off at top speed down the dark narrow stretch. When he got to the end there was not enough room to turn around, so he drove into a field and reversed.

A few weeks later Norman passed his test. Being able to drive opened a whole new world, he was no longer at the mercy of his friends. He could go and come just as he pleased. This new-found self-assurance was, however, little protection from the biting chill that enveloped the air. But his shivering body was warmed by the inner glow that he felt inside.

With deep grief we regret to announce the death of Claudia Jones, the revolutionary leader and Editor of the West Indian Gazette, on December 25 1964 at her home in Hampstead.

Miss Jones, who contracted a serious heart disease because of police persecutions, imprisonment in the USA and her hard struggle for more than 20 years in America for the freedom and equal rights of the Negro people, had a stroke on Christmas morning and passed away peacefully in her sleep.

WEST INDIAN GAZETTE JANUARY 1965

CHECKMATE FOR BISHOP

...fred Wood, Ina, with 3 of their 5 children.

Wilfred Wood becomes Britain's first black bishop

THE Church of England's first black bishop, Venerable Wilfred Wood vowed to continue to champion the cause of the downtrodden once he takes up his position.

The historic moment will take place in July where he will be consecrated by the Bishop of London, the Rt Ar-bishop of Canterbury, Robert Runcie, who will make him black bishop.

Wilfred Wood from Barbados was born in 1936 and boasts how it

Sobers, Wes Hall and the Mighty Sparrow blessed the earth with their presence.

On becoming Priest of St Paul's Cathedral he was made Arch Deacon of Southwark. In 1962. Married his childhood sweetheart Ina, he has five children.

Asked what he

that the Church of England was inclusive and that the clergy were basically white, middle-class and out of touch with the lives of or-dinary people he said:

"Christianity is stronger in this country than it has been, it was easier to have a valid thing to go to church because it could yield some sort of material advantage or social status. If you go to church today it can real-ly be only out of a ge-nuine conviction

longer a status ladder."

He went on to argue that he did not believe in the balance in the social make up of the church.

Religion is more interested in what you are. He is more interested in what you become rather than what you are.

Wilfred Wood, a known activist on many social justice committees, said he practised his principles at a tur-bulent time when he served as moderator of the World Council of

time controversy raged in 1979 when he reported with words and money the military strug-gle in Zimbabwe.

When asked how he felt about church involve-ment in politics par-ticularly in the background of pro-black statements by the Bishop of Durham, Dr Jenkins, he said: "The Bishop of Durham is the centre of great controversy and his views on christian leader worth his salt can would notice Christian

man.

You can't expect a church leader to obey to the about South Africa? It is clear that to struggle and fight is correct because the downtrodden are wronged."

The black community has changed radical-ly since the 50's and the younger generation have perhaps rejected much of traditional Christianity.

This is not despairing argues the Venerable Wilfred Wood. "As a

terms with itself and assure the identity of the past and this can be seen in the interest of Rastafarianism and so pentecostalism".

The position of Bishop was made vacant with the retirement of the Rt Rev Bishop the Venerable area Bishop Wilfred Wood will be responsible to the Bishop of Southwark Christian parishes in Croydon, Ad-dington, Coterham Gondstone, Reigate and

Dr Martin Luther King, the civil rights leader, was shot to death in Memphis, Tennessee, last night. Two unidentified men were arrested several blocks from where Dr King was shot while standing on his hotel balcony.

Four thousand National Guard troops were ordered into Memphis by the Governor. A curfew was imposed on the city of 550,000 with about 40 per cent Negro.
THE TIMES FRIDAY APRIL 5 1968

For Connie Goodridge, a few months in Jamaica turned into a few years. Her husband Stanley had promised to follow her, but despite the frequent letters insisting that he would "soon come", as the time passed Connie feared he had changed his mind.

One afternoon a letter arrived addressed to 'Mrs C Goodridge' in Stanley's scratchy writing. Eagerly Connie tore open the envelope. Her doubts became reality. He said he was sorry, but he felt it would be best if Connie returned to England with the children as soon as possible.

For days Connie cursed her husband and stubbornly vowed not to follow his request. She was happy in Jamaica, this was her home. Her family, friends and work was here. Thoughts of England only filled her with sadness.

But deep down Connie felt her actions were selfish. She had taken her marriage vows and promised to stay with her husband through the good times and bad times. There was also the children to consider. They were being deprived of their father.

Stanley Jnr was perfectly happy as he remembered nothing of England, but Amru had spent too much of her life in Britain and could not adjust to the Jamaican way. She constantly complained of the heat and the mosquitoes and could not understand the dialect. At the age of eight, she still could not read.

"I'm not a selfish person," Connie reasoned with her mother, as she began to pack up her belongings. The sour memories of long cold nights, paraffin heaters and humble dwellings came flooding back. But Connie was doing this for the family, not herself.

The night before Connie was due to leave, her brother in law came and begged her to leave Stanley Jnr in Jamaica with them. They loved him so much and could not bear the thought of being separated from him.

It was so difficult to leave without her baby, but Connie felt sure it was the right decision. She was not convinced that her husband had made proper provision for a wife and two children. No, Stanley Jnr would fair much better in Jamaica than in England, she decided.

Once again Connie said goodbye to her family. This time she knew it was for real.

Within weeks of returning to England, life for the Goodridge family was back to normal. Amru picked up and started to progress at school, Stanley was happy to have his family home and Connie threw herself relentlessly into work and finding somewhere decent to live. It was the only way she could deal with the pain of leaving Stanley Jnr in Jamaica.

Mr Enoch Powell was dismissed from his post as defence spokesman in the Shadow Cabinet last night. This followed his controversial speech on immigration at Birmingham on Saturday.

Mr Heath, leader of the Opposition, said he had told Mr Powell that he considered the speech to have

*been racialist in tone and liable to exacerbate racial
tension.*
THE TIMES MONDAY 21 APRIL 1968

"Councillor Powe, we don't think your actions last
night were appropriate. Councillors have a certain
unwritten code of conduct to follow and . . . "

Since becoming councillor in Long Eaton in 1963,
George Powe had fought for equality in terms of
better housing and better education. But it was an
uphill struggle against the racist remarks that were
flaunted around the council chamber.

The previous night, George's patience had been
stretched to breaking point. They had been
discussing a proposal for a family planning clinic to
serve inner city areas in a, mainly black, part of
Nottingham.

In the mist of the debate, one of the councillors
had turned to him and whispered that he should go
and tell his women to use contraception. George
looked the man dead in the eyes and told him that
he was not a doctor. The councillor leaned back in
his seat and loudly proclaimed that coloured women
bred like flies. Enraged, George got up and lunged
forward to thump him.

George had had enough. Their racist attitude
annoyed him, moreover black people found it very
difficult to get housing through the council. One
housing officer had even told him that he did not
mind housing a Jamaican, but would not consider
an African.

George decided that when his term was up, he
would not re-contest the Long Eaton seat. There were
other ways to fight the injustices of the system
through the creation of black-led organisations.

*Sir Learie Constantine, former test cricketer and one-
time High Commissioner in London for Trinidad and
Tobago, who is a member of the Race Relations
Board, is one of four new life peers named in the New
Years' Honours List. He will be the second non-
European to be a member of the House of Lords.*

*It is expected that Sir Learie, who is 67, will sit on
the x-bench without party allegiance. When the by-
election at Nelson and Colne was pending in May last
year, Mr Thorpe, the Liberal leader invited him to
stand as the Liberal candidate. Sir Learie refused and
it was generally understood that because of his
concern for fostering good relations between
Commonwealth immigrants and British people, he
preferred to abstain from party politics.*
THE TIMES JANUARY 1 1969

*Neil Armstrong became the first man to take a walk on
the moon's surface early today. This spectacular
moment came after he had inched his way down the
ladder of the fragile lunar bug, Eagle, while his
colleague Edwin Aldrin watched his movements from
inside the craft.*

*The landing was near perfect and the two
astronauts on board Eagle reported that it had not
tilted too far to prevent a take-off.*

*The first word from man on the moon came from
Aldrin: 'Tranquility base. The Eagle has landed.'*
THE TIMES JULY 21 1969

Mary George stroked her bulging stomach lovingly. It
was not long to go now, the baby was due in a few
weeks. She was uncomfortable and constantly
hungry, but worse of all she was bored.

For a couple of hours each day, she attempted to occupy her mind knitting cute little booties, or experimenting in the kitchen. But most of the time she opted to vegetate in front of the television.

Mary Johnson was working in Scotland when she received a letter from Paul suggesting they got engaged. This proposition was not good enough for Mary, she refused to be one of those girls who were in a continuous state of engagement, it was marriage or nothing.

A couple of months later one cold November morning, Miss Mary Johnson became Mrs Paul George. The wedding had been a quiet affair, just a few close friends in Wood Green registry office.

Mary was slightly disappointed that her father was not there to give her away, but he had written expressing his delight that she was marrying someone from the same island and whose family they knew.

After they were married Mary and Paul moved into a one bedroom flat in Winchmore Hill.

Anthony Joseph George, as his father named him, arrived at quarter past four in the afternoon. Mary thought that she would be happy to give birth to a healthy baby boy and be content in the knowledge that she achieved what she wanted in life, a career, a husband and a child.

The Home Office was last night studying a Special Branch preliminary report on the strength and activities of the Black Power Movement. The Home Secretary, Mr Maudling, called for the report after Sunday's clash between police and Black Panther demonstrators at Maida Vale. Police regard Black Power as worthy of extremely tight surveillance.

The Secretary of the West Indian Standing

Conference, Mr Jeff Crawford, warned yesterday that policemen might be killed if action was not taken to end conflict between black youth and police. Mr Crawford said this was not an extremist minority view. Black people generally feared violence was inevitable because they were being harassed by police and felt hopelessness over the redress of complaints. THE GUARDIAN AUGUST 12 1970

FIFTY WINTERS ON

Gloria Bailey *(Born in Jamaica in 1929. Came to the UK in 1954 and has since fostered over fifty children. Now spends her time doing community and charity work.)*

"Although my parents did not want me to come to England, when I went back to the Caribbean for a visit, my mum could see I had made the right decision. She was so happy that I looked well and that her grandchildren were doing fine.

"I think if I had stayed in Jamaica I would not have been able to educate my children to the level that I did, because it is quite expensive to educate children over there. My daughter Beverley has a degree in English from Cambridge and is a teacher. She was the first black Education Officer at Belmarsh Prison. Now she's doing her PhD. Grace is a health adviser. Sonny is an assistant manager at Cable and Wireless and Charles is a songwriter.

"I left my job with a telecommunications company to become a full-time foster mum. My boss thought I was crazy, but I love children. Since 1984 I have fostered over fifty children. I still have two at the moment. Funnily enough they are two white children, and they've been with me for over ten years. People thinks it's strange, but I was the only person who would take them. They're happy here and are really thriving.

"I like to go on holiday to Jamaica, but England is my home now. Why move from here and have to start all over again? Most of the people I knew in the Caribbean have either emigrated or, sadly, passed away."

Ben Bousquet *(Arrived in the UK in 1956 from his native St. Lucia. A political activist, he is a former local councillor and a founding member of Black Sections in the Labour Party. Recently recruited as a consultant on BBC TV's 'Windrush' series.)*

"I had always planned to return to St Lucia to enter politics. My family had a strong political background. But it is too late now, I missed my opportunity. I have no doubt in my mind that I would have had a lot to contribute politically to St Lucia. I don't think it's fair to go back now. A new generation of politicians have taken over.

"I have got my house here in England, so this must be my home. I have some loyalty here because it gave me a life to which I am accustomed. By the same token, I can't forget my roots or the people I grew up with. Friends, my teachers, my whole life was shaped by the people who I met in my formative years in St Lucia.

"I go back every year. One day I may just pack up my bags and go back permanently.

"Any person from the Caribbean or Africa living in this country who has worked hard and has reached an age where they have obtained their pensions and want to return home should be able to do so. But many of them haven't enough money to do so.

"I spend quite a lot of my time in South Africa. I spent a whole year there and I helped to organise the last elections in 1995. I was given an area in the Transvaal where I returned a 96 per cent vote. I am very proud of my anti-apartheid work.

"I want to write a series of books, with my best friend Colin Douglas, for a political strategy for black people to follow. I believe that black people should make their voices heard in every institution.

"My fear for the younger generations is that they are not organised politically, so society doesn't pay any attention to them. They need to organise themselves within the system."

T Cooper *(Born in Jamaica. He arrived in Britain in 1948 at the age of 23 on the Empire Windrush and worked as a tailor for many years.)*
"England is not the Motherland. I feel, like many, let down. There was not as much as a hand stretched out to help us. A lot of us didn't come to spend more than five years, but fifty years later we are still here. At school we used to sing 'Land of Hope and Glory', then I came to England and found out what that actually meant.

"I don't think I would have come to England if I could make the decision again. We came here when we were young, sacrificed the best years of our lives, but not many of us made anything of ourselves.

"I have three children and they all want to go back to Jamaica, even though they were born here. But there's not really that much for them there. It's really good for people my age to go back, but not for young people.

"I'm going back any day now. We have been planning it for a couple of years. As pensioners we'll be better off over there. I'm looking forward to the sun. I'm going to be out in the country raising chickens, picking fruit and all those kind of things. My brothers went back home some years ago. I'll be going to join them.

"My kids complain that they suffered because they did not get much love when they were growing up, as we always had to work and in the evening we would be too tired to spend quality time with them.

"I've never seen myself as British. I don't think my children see themselves as British either. I don't think that time will ever come. Even other cultures who come here, I doubt they ever feel British.

"The fiftieth anniversary of the Empire Windrush is something to be celebrated. It will bring back memories, but I think it is sad that most of the people who were on that pioneering voyage with me have died, gone back home or have disappeared."

Len Garrison

"Leaving Jamaica did expand one's visions and thoughts. But we also lost the spirit of togetherness and sense of belonging. I don't think we will ever be valued here. Perhaps we are richer materially, but we are poorer spiritually. Young people growing up don't have the sort of bond that we had in the Caribbean. I see that with my own family. Even the concept of community is losing its value.

"The notion of Britishness is even losing meaning for white people, much less black people.

"We need to define ourselves as Africans in a British context and develop that into a sense of identity. Just like the Jews, wherever they are, they have a Jewishness but they also develop a national concept for that Jewishness.

"I think my greatest achievements here have been helping the community. I am director of the Association of Caribbean Families Education and Cultural Centre in Nottingham."

Cecil Holness *(Born 27 December, 1922 in Jamaica. Now retired and lives in Tooting, south London.)*

"Being in the RAF helped a lot of us from the Caribbean to settle down in Britain, both financially and educationally. It gave us the chance. It also helped us adjust socially. To be truthful, we more or less worshipped the white people we had back home at the time. They were top at everything and you would never expect to hear a white man swear or see him gambling or doing anything out of order. It was drilled into us at school that England was the mother country and that we were 'British subjects'. We were taught a lot about English history, and we were so patriotic about this country that, with England in war, we felt that it was only right that we came over and did our bit to help, even if it meant sacrificing our lives. I was very excited about coming over and actually seeing Hampton Court and all those places. In my school days I even wanted to be an Englishman, because of the way they spoke and dressed. To me they seemed to be gentlemanly. But after arriving here, I was disappointed.

"The RAF even got us used to bacon and eggs, even though most of us wanted breadfruit for breakfast.

"England still remains the motherland for me because it has given me so many opportunities, even if we didn't always get the appreciation we deserved.

"One day, during the war, I was hitchhiking from Colchester to London, dressed in my RAF uniform, and I was picked up by this Englishman and his wife in a Bentley. They thanked me for coming over. When we reached the outskirts of London, I said, any Underground station will do. However, the man insisted on driving me to my destination, and thanked me again.

"But after the war was over, the first thing everyone asked was, 'When are you going back to your own country?' Their thinking was that England had won the war and that they could now do without us.

"A lot of us had great hopes and dreams, which some of us achieved. Some saw England as a chance to work and save and go back home and start some sort of business. Whereas others wanted to get further education.

"Most of us can say that this country has done something for us. There were no jobs in Jamaica. If it wasn't for this country giving us the opening and opportunity, we would not have been able to buy a car, let alone a house.

"I feel that some of our own people don't do enough to assimilate with English people. Some of us impose our own little colour bar, and refuse to mix. I first noticed that in the RAF. Most West Indian servicemen kept together and made no effort to eat or socialise with the white boys. We have to learn about the English and they have to learn about us. They say that we are dirty, but we are cleaner than them. In the RAF, the black servicemen showered every night before going to bed, whereas the white servicemen just washed around their necks and went to bed. I'm a black man and my foot is black, but my foot is cleaner than his. The white boys had a shower or bath Friday night, because that was when we got clean laundry, then they didn't bother again during the week. Some of them were even sarcastic, saying, 'Oh, you don't want to wash so often, because the dirt doesn't show up on you.' Back home, you would never leave the house without taking a quick shower. If you didn't have a shower, you got your little bath pan in the yard and filled it with water and poured it over yourself. So I said to the boys, we've got to teach these white people, because a lot of them know very little about the West Indians. Even today, I find that the Englishman still knows very little about us.

"I never regret staying in Britain all these years, but I always stay in touch with my little Jamaica. Since I first came here in the summer of 1944, I've been back to Jamaica nine times."

Olympic javelin gold medallist Tessa Sanderson, collected a medal of a different kind last week. She went to Buckingham Palace to collect her MBE from the Queen.
THE VOICE MARCH 23 1985

Mary George *(Born in Antigua in 1944 and came to Britain as a teenager in 1962. She still works as a midwife.)*
"If I could make the same decision I would do it all over again. My life has turned out fairly well and I wouldn't like to change anything.

"I can't say I've gained or I've lost by coming here. If I had stayed in the Caribbean my life would probably have been jut as fulfilling, but in a different way.

"Wherever my children were born I think they would have turned out the same. It's my values that have shaped them, rather than the environment. When I look at my siblings in the West Indies, they have the same values, as do their children.

"One of my biggest regrets about being in Britain, is that I was not around when my father died in the Caribbean. I had seen him a couple of years before but I felt as if I never said goodbye.

"It would have been nice to have one of my siblings here in England, but that's life.

"I want to go back home to be able to sit on the beach and see the sea. Financially we will be better off as the British pension goes further there. I'm

hoping it will be more of a relaxed life. If I was to
retire here I think I would spend more time indoors.
Back home you don't have to think about heating the
house or the cold weather."

*A black youth strides down the riot torn streets of
Handsworth in Birmingham, a lighted petrol bomb in
his hand. In a nearby street a policeman shelters
behind his shield on the second day of a war in the
streets of Britain's second city which has left two
dead, two others missing and shops petrol bombed
and looted.*
THE MIRROR SEPTEMBER 11 1985

Trevor Kerr *(Came to Britain in 1953 as a 15-year-
old. He lives in south London and works making
artificial limbs.)*
"If I had my choice, I would have had all my children
educated in Jamaica, because they don't get on as
well here. What's wrong with the system? Everyone
blames one another instead of doing something
about the problem.

"When I came here couldn't believe the way that
people spoke to their parents, it has got worse now.

"Every time I go back home my eyes fill up with
water, even now. I always wanted to go back
permanently. Family and my house have kept me
here, but when I retire I'm going home straight away.

"Coming here was an eye-opener. In Jamaica I
had servants. Over here I had to wash my own
clothes for the first time.

"I am a Jamaican and a proud Jamaican. That's
one thing people can't take away from me. People say
Jamaica is a bad place, but I don't care what people
say it's one of the prettiest islands in the world, and

that will never change.

"I think my children have lost out from not being in Jamaica. All of my daughter's friends are either Jamaican or of West Indian parentage, which is a good thing because she knows her culture. She has heard me talk so much about Jamaica, sometimes she talks Jamaican patois like me.

"One thing that I'm very sorry about is that the Government doesn't allow you to chastise your children. In Jamaica, if your child is out of order you can beat him anytime you want and nobody can do anything about it. Discipline for children in this country is lacking.

"If I could live my life over I wouldn't have come to England. No way, no way, not with what I know now. But it took me a long time to find out. I think I should have gone to Florida with my brothers, one of them is now a millionaire.

Connie Marks *(75-years-old. Born in Kingston, Jamaica. Came to Britain aged 31 in November 1954. Now lives in Ladbroke Grove, London, from where she campaigns to preserve the house of the legendary black nurse Mary Seacole, as a national monument.)* "Young people should respect the way us older people are. Young people ask me if I like being called black. No I don't. I prefer to be called coloured. If for forty-five years of your life you are called Michael then on your forty-sixth birthday people decide to call you Samuel, you won't like it. Young black people must accept that. I like going to South Africa because I am called coloured. Well, most of my life I have been called coloured. And that's what I am.

"Some people call themselves African Americans, I don't want to be called no damn African Caribbean. Call me a Jamaican. That's where I was born. My birth certificate says nothing about African. I do have African blood in me, but I have other bloods too- Scottish, Indian, Lebanese. So why must I just hang on black and African?

"I lead an active life. I give talks to children in school on life in Jamaica and my experiences here in the early years. I do a lot of charity work in South Africa and I do quite a lot of media work nowadays."

Robert Murray *(Was born in 1923 in British Guiana. Initially came to Britain to fight for 'king and country' during World War II. Now retired, he lives in Derby where he pursues his interest in writing.)*
"There came a point when you knew you are going to die here. I have been in Britain longer than I have been at home. I could not go back now. I did go back, after thirty years, but I was not at all impressed. After the first week I wanted to come back to England. You grow accustomed to the ways of this country. I'm more accustomed to the cold than the heat. I see this as my home. I think our parents knew that when they said goodbye to their sons and daughters, they weren't coming back."

Norman Phillips *(Aged 68. Came to England from Trinidad in 1955. Now lives in Finsbury Park, north London)*
"The majority of us thought we'd work, try and save a little money and get back to the Caribbean. We never knew it was impossible because we were going to have families and problems and it was going to take years.

"Even though the island I came from was poor, I miss everything about it, because I left everything and everybody there to come over here. Life was so sweet and simple when you could climb a tree and pick a coconut. Life was so easy when you could cut a sugar cane by the roadside whenever you needed one. When you could go by the river and sit there and have a bath and swim and catch two fish.

"When you could plant a little cassava and some peas. Life was sweet because everyone was loving and jolly. No-one had wicked or nasty thoughts about anyone else. You lost all of that the moment you landed in Britain.

"I was told that this was the Motherland and that we would get employment. I had no guidance and feel deceived. Because I was in paradise and lost it.

"The most important way forward for the future is education. Remember, they used to hide books away from black people in my grandparents' day, they wanted us to stay illiterate. Once you have knowledge you have power.

"I'm dying to go back to Trinidad. I'm making plans already. I believe the best part of my life will be the end of it. Because I'll be living in a place where I don't have to sweat to pay bills. Paradise island, beach, sunshine, beautiful rain, all my fruits to eat and loving black people around me.

"But until then, I'm trapped here. This cold air is killing me, I've had enough of this country, man.

"I think it's been a waste of time coming to England. I should have been happy enough with my parents and stayed with them. My mother died, my father died, my sister died and I can't find my little sister now. So coming here has only mashed me up. The only thing I have in this country is my children.

"If you go to the bookie shops, you want to see how many of the first generation are in there. They can't get a job, because they are too old, but don't have the money to go home. The man in the bookies has even put seats in there for them now.

"I went back to college because I realised that as a labourer I was a nobody. I thought, if I was going back to the Caribbean I needed to have a few skills. Now I can make furniture and make money. I can sew and mend a sewing machine. I know that when I go home I can't suffer.

"After many years working as a labourer, in December 1995 I was awarded a degree in plumbing. It's a skill that I'll be able to take back with me to the Caribbean."

Britain's new Black MPs have hailed their historic wins as a new era in black politics. Bernie Grant, Tottenham's new MP predicted that "black people would be dancing in the streets' after hearing that Paul Boateng, Keith Vaz and Diane Abbott would join him as Britain's first black MPs since World War II.
THE VOICE JUNE 16 1987

Charlie Phillips *(Came to Britain from Jamaica in 1955 when he was only thirteen. He now owns an award-winning restaurant, Smokey Joe's Diner, in Wandsworth.)*
"Given the choice again, I would still have come over. I see myself as Jamaican and British. When in Rome do as the Romans do. I try to fit in, wherever I am I just blend in. I have gained experience from being here. Career-wise I wouldn't have achieved so much in Jamaica, I came from a lower working class family.

"As a photographer in the seventies I was successful in Italy, France and Switzerland. I was the first black photographer for Italian Vogue in 1971. I worked as a paparazzi taking pictures of stars like Jimi Hendrix and Sophia Loren. Some of my photos are in the National Portrait Gallery.

"I have never forgotten my roots, yet I won't go back to Jamaica permanently. I let my children know about my humble beginnings in a tenement yard in Kingston. I remember the days of hunger. It's my roots and I'm not ashamed of it.

"I feel the black community is more segregated now, which makes me sad. When we first came here we used to do things together and people would help one another. We used to have a system called 'pardner' whereby we could save up for the deposits on our homes collectively. The Government used to wonder how come so many black people could buy their own houses. But now people don't really trust one another and consequently we don't have a strong financial footing.

"Young people need to be entrepreneurs to survive. They need education and to be street-wise. That's what I tried to teach my two sons."

Patricia Scotland is Britain's first black woman Queen's Counsel. She took Silk at the House of Commons recently with her proud parents Dellie and Arthur Clark in attendance.
THE VOICE APRIL 16 1991

Captain Fish
Aston Ferguson *(Came to the UK at the age of 19. He is currently a Staff Sargeant in the British Army and organizes, amongst other things, the annual Royal Tournament at Earl's Court.)*
Invited to Britain from Kingston, Jamaica, in 1961, as performers to sing, limbo dance, jive and entertain. Their five-man troupe was called Captain Fish and his Limbo Dancers. Ferguson was only 19-

years-old at the time, while Fish was the top dancer in Jamaica.

"A hotel manager told us about a spot in England, and that if we were interested it was ours. We were excited, everyone had told us Britain was a land of gold. We appeared on Come Dancing and Opportunity Knocks and we danced with Millie Small, Jackie Edwards, Ray Charles and James Brown," said Aston. "We even performed at the Royal Albert Hall with Sammy Davis Jnr, Cleo Lane and Dick Gregory.

"When we arrived in England it was freezing. It was the first time that I saw overcoats and I thought, what are men doing wearing skirts? It was September and in those days winter used to come early, not like now. From August you had to start wearing your coat because it was freezing.

"We initially hitched up with friends, you shared until you could afford to get your own room. We used to sleep three in a bed. The white people wouldn't rent us rooms.

"Meanwhile, back home, my folks were expecting weekly letters with a little money. I didn't want to disappoint them, so I worked hard and always managed to send something.

"We thought that we were earning good money, but when we started to hear how much the white artists were getting, we realised we were being robbed. £60 per show between the five of us. But it was take it or leave it. There were not many black artists around at the time. The first black artist to really make it over here was Danny Williams, a South African, singing 'Moon River'. He came over and he was big for a time.

"Limbo was new at the time in this country and everyone flocked to see us. Even some black people had never seen limbo. Back home, limbo

performances were really confined to tourists. We did
a lot of shows for pure black folk. Sometimes we'd
have three different gigs a night. Drive up to Wales
and do an early show then drive back to the West
End that night and do another, then get up for work
in the morning. We worked hard here, boy.

"Soon the white people took over the limbo
dancing scene and taught it to the kids. Suddenly
everyone was doing limbo dancing. Then, after a
year, it was dead completely. After that we had to
concentrate on our trade."

During this time Aston worked as an electrician at
the Sunlight Laundry in Fulham, while Fish worked
at Morgan Carbonites, eventually staying there for
twenty-seven years.

"When we appeared on Come Dancing," said
Captain Fish, "the people were asking what the hell
we were doing there, we were the only black people.
But after we'd performed they didn't want us to come
off the stage. We were the warm up act for The
Beatles on their UK tour.

"I thought I would only stay in England for five
years. But the economy at home was not getting any
better."

George Powe (*Born in 1926. He came to the UK from
Jamaica in 1943 to fight for 'king and country' in
World War II. Formerly a local councillor, he is the
founding member of a Nottingham based community
group.*)
"It's very difficult to say whether I would make the
same decision to come here, if I could turn back the
clock. Coming here I did gain a lot of experience, I
understand more clearly how the white people think
and act. I have also realised how many black people
threw our race down the drain. I go back to Jamaica

every year, but it's too late to go back permanently,"

Doris Rankin *(Born 1915, in Portland, Jamaica. Now retired and lives in Tottenham, north London.)*
"I have adjusted myself to the English way of life, but I support the reparations movement that people like Tottenham MP Bernie Grant are calling for. The Government should pay a good lump sum for us to settle back home

"If my mum and dad were still alive I would have ended up going back to Jamaica. But I have never been back. I have a big family over here. I still have memories about how lovely Jamaica was. The fragrance, the sun, the trees, the rivers and sea. My grandchildren who have been there say to me, 'Gran, I don't know why you came over here?' They complain that two weeks in Jamaica isn't enough time for them, and they keep going back on holiday.

Andre Shervington *(Came to Britain from British Guiana to serve 'king and country' in World War II. After leaving the RAF he stayed on in the UK and made a career in the civil service. Died in May 1998.)*
"Notting Hill has always been a truly mixed and integrated area. I would like to believe that that is what has kept me here, but I'm not sure.

"I've enjoyed every carnival from the first to the most recent. What makes carnival beautiful is the smiles you see on the faces of people there.

"I have achieved piece of mind, I feel very safe. I've got older and I'm not being persecuted like I used to be persecuted by the police, but the struggle continues. I'm very happy with the way the second generation have taken on the struggle, but I want to see more of it. This generation is breaking down the

barriers and the generations after that will break
them down even further. Optimism does not come
into it, I know what the result will be. They will
either have to kick us all out or treat us as normal
people.

"But I don't want to see my West Indian people
going around hating anybody, because hate is a fatal
disease. I want to see them try to love even their
enemies.

"I'm now 74. I have loving children, a loving wife
and loving grandchildren, that' s all I want in life. I
never wanted to be this or that. All I came to Britain
for was to learn a craft, which I did and was
successful with it.

"If I could turn back the clock I wouldn't have
lived in England after the war, I would have lived in
France. I find them a much more civilised people.
There was no other option at the time, because we
were born British and were not aware of our history.

"I can't go back to the Caribbean, that would be a
regressive step. I went back to Guyana twice hoping
to remain, but found out that I could not. I don't
blame people for going back. You've got this thing
inside you that draws you back. You've got to go
there and try to get it out of your system. It's out of
my system because I've done it twice. I know so
many people who have made the mistake of building
a home in the Caribbean and gone back and have
had to return to England when their money is all
gone.

"I am no longer a nationalist. To me, the world is
my oyster. I encourage younger people to travel and
broaden their horizons. They are living in Europe, so
get to know Europe, don't be afraid to travel
anywhere because the only difference between them
and another European is the colour of their skin.
You speak a European language, you've got a

European education, so use it."

Pastor Io Smith *(Came to Britain from Jamaica in 1957 when she was 19-years-old. Now pastor of the pentecostal church in Leytonstone.)*
"For those of us that pulled through, it was hardship, the racism we suffered was blatant. Those who came later and those who were born here don't realise that the way had been paved for them.

"One of my proudest moments was when I was awarded an MBE in 1994 for the work that I have done. I have founded two homes for the elderly, a mental illness project, a day-care centre, a fund to help educate poor children in Jamaica, I offer counselling to young people, and set up a school in Ghana for orphans. All I want from life now is to be able to reside back in Jamaica. But I've no plans because there is so much to do right here."

Kelvin Cook-Mohammed *(Born 1926, Port of Spain, Trinidad. Came to England in 1956 to try his luck. Worked as an accountant. Now retired and lives in Finsbury Park, north London)*
"I really wanted to emigrate to the States or Canada, but in those days it wasn't so easy. The alternative was to try for England and I had a cousin over here. I wanted to travel and I can't stand the excessive heat of Trinidad. I was hoping to stay in England for a long time depending on how things went. I wanted to do accounts. When I arrived in Liverpool it was drizzling and dark, I wanted to go back. Nevertheless I took the train to London and was met by my cousin and aunt. I went straight to a Catholic international student hostel in Holland Park. I had been in correspondence with a priest there. I just spent my first night there.

The next day I went to the home of a family of students from East Africa. That was in Clapham South.

"I went to agencies to look for a job in accounting. I had no problems getting a job. The first one I found was with the Automobile Association in Leicester Square. I was there for some years. I liked England because I was able to meet people from all different countries. I did not really miss home that much. I think it was because I was in regular contact with my family. Several of them came over to visit.

"I'm very adaptable, so getting accustomed to life here was fine. The Underground took a little getting used to. My first journey on the tube was to Clapham South station, shortly after I arrived. I felt scared to go so deep in the ground. I was worried about what happened if it flooded. The smog was also unfamiliar. Sometimes it was so thick you couldn't see your hand in front of your face. I remember one night, it was so bad I had trouble finding my house.

"Like a lot of young people at the time, I hung out in coffee bars, one particularly near Victoria train station. I used to go to the Empire Ball Room and Cafe de Paris in the West End for dancing. When I worked in Leicester Square they used to have cheap dancing at lunch time at the Cafe de Paris. One shilling for lunch time dancing. A few of us from the office would go there. That was a nice way to pass the time. They would play rock and roll and cha-cha-cha. It was a mixture of records and live bands. Shirley Bassey and Tommy Steele were popular. She rehearsed in a building near our office. Then there was actress/singer Sabrina, S44 (that was her nickname, as she was well-endowed, and also her car reg.) We went to cartoon cinemas and newsreels regularly, where we'd pay about a shilling and watch continuous news or cartoons. In the summer we'd go down to the Embankment at lunch time and sit on the grass by the

Thames and listen to live bands.

"Here, at dances, women would dance with other women, which just didn't happen in Trinidad. Neither could we understand the pub culture. Whenever there was something to celebrate in the office we would always go to the pub. What I could not understand was, when it was someone's anniversary or birthday, they bought the cake for everyone else to eat.

"Pubs didn't exist in Trinidad. It was almost unacceptable for men and women to be drinking together. There were rum shops but they were for the men.

"I can't say that I have ever experienced any racial or colour problems in my years in Britain. If I have, I didn't notice them.

"Went back to Trinidad in 1980s but it was too hot. I have been here more years than I was in Trinidad. I see myself as a Trinidadian living in Britain, even though I have lived here so long I always stress the Trinidadian connection. But things have changed too much for me to go back to Trinidad."

Winston Stafford-Husband *(Born in Barbados in 1942. Has worked for London Transport since arriving in the UK in 1961.)*
"I believe I will eventually end up back home. I'm waiting on the wife . . . When she ready, I ready. I think I benefited from coming here and opened door for others. I've no regrets about coming here, then again I'm probably too old to regret anything.

"Knowing what I know now, I still would have come to England. But I would have quit working for London Transport a long time ago and looked for a job elsewhere."

Clarence Thompson *(Born in Trinidad and Tobago in 1940. came to the UK in 1960. He is a former general-secretary of the West Indian Standing Conference and is currently a manager at British Petroleum. He lives in south-east London.)*

"I have exceeded my ambitions in Britain. If I had stayed in Trinidad all this would probably not have happened.

"I wrote a poem, 'Pathway to Freedom' to commemorate the United Nation's campaign of sanctions against apartheid South Africa. I was invited to recite the poem in the House of Lords in the eighties and invited to Jamaica by the then Prime Minister, Michael Manley. I am now general secretary of the West Indian Standing Conference, which works towards improving the lives and conditions for black people here in Britain.

"But, of course, there are things that I feel sad about life in England. Particularly the Immigration Acts. When Maggie Thatcher came to power she said that Britain was being swamped by 'an alien culture', and our automatic right to a British passport was taken away.

"I also feel very bitter about black deaths in police custody. All we have heard is excuses as to why people have died.

"I don't see Britain as the Motherland. No mother kills its babies and legitimizes the killing. Any mother that does this and continues to do this must be insane. What I have achieved here is down to me not due to anything that was given to me.

"We have achieved in Britain, in spite of the difficulties we found here. We achieved excellence in adversity. It shows the strength of black people."

SIGNIFICANT DATES

1948
British Nationality Act gives all Commonwealth people right to British citizenship.

Arrival of Empire Windrush from Jamaica with 500 West Indians. Arrival seen as the start of post-war immigration from the Caribbean.

1950
CY GRANT sings the news in calypso on British television.

1952
McCarren-Walter Act restricts immigration to United States, and United Kingdom becomes choice destination for West Indians seeking employment.

Trinidadian sprinter EMMAUNEL MACDONALD BAILEY is first black athlete to win an Olympic medal competing for Great Britain.

1951
Jamaican DAILY GLEANER newspaper launched in London.

1956

PEARL CONNOR-MOGOTSI establishes the first black
theatre agency in London.

London Transport begins recruiting staff in Barbados.

1958
Black American activist CLAUDIA JONES sets up WEST
INDIAN GAZETTE, a monthly newspaper, in Brixton,
London.

Nottingham and Notting Hill experience riots as white
youths go on the rampage against black immigration.
Riots strengthen anti-immigration feeling in
Parliament. Tory MP Cyril Osbourne calls for tougher
immigration controls.

Trinidadian EDRIC CONNOR becomes first black actor to
act with the Royal Shakespeare Company.

1962
The Commonwealth Immigrants Bill 1962, restricts
entry of settlers to those with employment vouchers.

Jamaica becomes the first Caribbean island to gain
independence from Britain.

1964
First Notting Hill Carnival held.

Peter Griffiths, Tory MP for Smethwick fights election
on an openly racist platform using slogan, "If you want
a nigger for a neighbour, vote Labour."

1965
White Paper on Commonwealth immigrants issued
from the Labour Government. It aims to reduce the
level of immigration.

Race Relations Act makes discrimination on the basis of colour, race, ethnicity or national origin illegal.

1966
Local Government Act provides funding for local authorities to help ethnic minority groups.

First black officer joins Metropolitan Police Force.

London Transport recruits in Trinidad and Tobago, and Jamaica.

1967
Paul Stephenson is the first black man on the British Sports Council and establishes the Mohammed Ali Sports Development Association.

Caribbean born Dudley Dryden and Len Dyke set up a cosmetics business in London which eventually becomes a multimillion pound company.

1968
The Commonwealth Immigrants Act further tightens entry, but a clause retains free entry for ex-colonials with white skin.

Race Relations Bill extends scope of earlier bill, includes housing, education and employment.

MP Enoch Powell warns of racial violence if immigration continues, in his "Rivers of Blood" speech.

1969
Trinidadian Sir Learie Constantine becomes a peer in the House of Lords.

1971
Immigration Act ends primary immigration.

UK Afro-Caribbean population now at half a million.

1974 ALEX PASCALL presents the first black radio programme, Black Londoners, on the BBC.

1975
Grenadian born DR DAVID PITT becomes the first black chair of the Greater London Council.

Black feature film, Pressure, is financed and made by HORACE OVE and SAM SELVON. The film is banned as authorities fear its impact.

1976
Race Relations Act extends the scope of earlier legislation to cover indirect racism. Race watchdog, Commission for Racial Equality, formed.

1978
Lambeth Council establishes Britain's first race relations unit.

DESMOND DOUGLAS becomes the top British table tennis player.

First black soap, Empire Road, aired on British television.

VIV ANDERSON becomes the first black footballer to be picked for England's national squad.

CHARLES MUNGO is appointed first black secondary school headmaster.

1979

ARTHUR LEWIS becomes the first black economics professor in Britain and wins Nobel Prize for Economics.

1980

RONALD HOPE becomes the first black police inspector in the UK.

1981

Metropolitan Police launch Swamp '81.

Rioting in Brixton, Toxteth and Moss Side as tension reaches breaking point between the police and black youth.

1982

Jamaican born VAL MCCALLA launches THE VOICE newspaper, which becomes Britain's largest selling black newspaper.

1984

LYDIA SIMMONS becomes the first female black Mayor in Britain.

1985

Riots in Handsworth, Birmingham.

Riots in Brixton following the shooting of CHERRY GROCE during a police raid on her home.

PC Keith Blakelock killed in Tottenham riots.

1987

JANET ADEGOKE becomes first black female mayor of London borough of Hammersmith and Fulham

JOHN BARNES first black footballer to be awarded Professional Footballers Player of the Year trophy.

RICHARD STOKES becomes first black man to join Royal Guards.

Four black Labour MPs elected to parliament.

1988
Barbados born accountant JIM BRAITHWAITE sets up multi-million pound computer firm, the first black company to be listed on the Stock Exchange.

LEONARD WOODLEY and JOHN ROBERTS are first black QCs to take silk.

NAOMI CAMPBELL, first black British supermodel, becomes the highest paid.

1990
JIM WILLIAMS becomes first black Lord Mayor of Bristol.

London's first legal urban music radio station Choice FM starts broadcasting.

1992
BILL MORRIS becomes the first black leader of Britain's largest trade union, the Transport and General Workers Union.

STEVE POPE and DOTUN ADEBAYO start a black writing revolution, when their company, THE X PRESS, launches its first book, Victor Headley's *Yardie*, which becomes and instant bestseller.

1993

PAUL INCE becomes first black player to Captain England team.

Teenager STEPHEN LAWRENCE murdered in a racist attack in South East London.

Britain's first black cable channel Identity Television launched.

1995
Metropolitan Police Commissioner Sir Paul Condon launches operation Eagle Eye. His comments that 70 per cent of street crime is caused by black people sparks controversy.

1997
Labour Home Secretary Jack Straw launches Crime and Disorder Bill designed to strengthen laws against racial violence and harassment.

REVEREND JOEL EDWARDS becomes first black man appointed as general director of the Evangelical Alliance.

OONA KING becomes Labour's fourth black MP.

1998
Financier CARL CUSHNIE becomes the first Afro-Caribbean to join the ranks of Britain's richest 500 citizens.

In Search of Satisfaction by J. California Cooper
'One of America's greatest black female writers' is just one of the many accolades that have been heaped upon the writing phenomenon called J. California Cooper. Only now is she been discovered in Britain but Americans in the know have been signing her praises for some time. Her list of work includes 'A Piece of Mine', 'Homemade Love', 'Some Soul to Keep', 'Family' and 'The Matter is life'

Nia have bought the UK rights to three of her best works and In Search of Satisfaction is the first of her works to be released in Britain.

In Search of Satisfaction is a powerful human drama of two families linked by the same man. Josephus's daughter Ruth is born to a hard working mother and seems destined to a life of poverty. Yinyang, is Josephus's daughter by his alcoholic mistress. In seeking the legacy left by their father, both end up pulling themselves and their families onto an emotional roller coaster.

ISBN 1-874509-41-7

The Judas Factor by Karl Evanzz

Discover the startling truth behind the assassination of the most powerful and controversial black leader of the 20th century.

ON FEBRUARY 21, 1965, Malcolm X was shot and killed. Now, based on fifteen years of research, including hundreds of interviews and the examination of 300,000 pages of declassified FBI and CIA documents, *The Judas Factor* provides the first in-depth analysis of the role the intelligence community played in instigating the death of the Nation of Islam's most revered and feared leader.

The Judas Factor details Malcolm X's rise and fall, revealing how the intelligence community monitored him, through agents provocateur and infiltration, manipulating his course. Thoroughly documented, *The Judas Factor* is a rivetting and often shocking work that sheds new light on the tragic death of one of the greatest black leaders of our time.

Karl Evanzz is an award winning freelance writer whose articles have appeared in numerous publications. He currently works for the Washington Post.

ISBN 1-874509-59-X

Keep updated with the literary gems from Nia
Join our mailing list.
Simply send your name and address to:

Mailing List
Nia
6 Hoxton Square
London N1 6NU

The Dotun Adebayo Show
Every Tuesday evening
10.30pm - 1.00am
on BBC GLR 94.9FM (London)

Time to hear what you've been missing.